"Tell the truth. Tell the truth with your whole body.
Don't spare the reader. You tell it.
We killed plenty of people. I mean me. Me. Me.
Tell the terror and horror of it. The total waste of it.
Put the truth in your reader's hands. Write a letter.
Tell the truth to a real person here in front of you.
She wants to hear your story. Tell it to her.
I want to hear your story. Tell it to me."

Larry Heinemann, Vietnam Veteran, Author

AFTER ACTION REVIEW

A Collection of Writing and Artwork
by Veterans of the Global War on Terror

WARRIORWriters

Published by Warrior Writers
Email: info@warriorwriters.org
Website: www.warriorwriters.org

Printed by L. Brown and Sons Printing, Inc.
14-20 Jefferson Street
Barre, Vermont 05641

ISBN - 978-0-615-56151-6

Edited by Lovella Calica
Design and Typeset by Rachel McNeill

This book is dedicated to Johnny Millantz.
A friend to many of us, the
joy in his laughter lives deep within us.
Johnny, we are forever
grateful for your heart and we miss you.

July 30, 1981 - April 3, 2009

"People who care what we have to say surround us. They draw the stories out of us by their wanting to know."

Maxine Hong Kingston, Author,
Warrior Writers Advisory Board

TABLE OF CONTENTS

WALKING UPON THE HOLY LAND

THE BLOW OF MEMORY'S RETURN

CONSTANTLY CHASING CATHARSIS

SOWING COMMUNITY

Cover and section artwork is from the "Dust Memories" collection by Aaron Hughes, a series of drawings, paintings, and collages that communicates the ambiguous and anxious moments of his deployment with the 1244th Transportation Company in Iraq. Aaron describes the collection as a "repeating cycle" and metaphor for his continually repeating thoughts of the experience and the reality that this journey is still being carried out today by soldiers in Iraq. The following works are included: "MSR Tampa South II" (cover), "Camp Champion" (title page), "Talil Airbase" (9), "Camel Herder" (55), "Dead Desert Dust" (95), and "MSR Tampa I" (119).

Photos of artwork and veterans were taken by Lovella Calica, unless otherwise noted.

WARRIOR WRITERS IS...

Warrior Writers is a community
a discovery
an exploration
a movement
a book, a performance
a voice, a declaration
a sound that keeps getting louder and clearer

Warrior Writers is a feeling, a culture, a history
a community
a voice
a place for voices
it is asking
it is telling
listening, learning
reaching deeper
growing stronger
more clear
a statement
a question
What is Warrior Writers to you?

It has been almost five years since the first Warrior Writers workshop in New York City on a cold February morning. What started out as an idea has become a movement of veterans carving out space for creative voices, experiences, and reflections.

Warrior Writers has become a home, a vehicle, an understanding, a way to relate to others. Warrior Writers exists to be a place where we can come to not only reflect on our experiences through art, but a place to move on, to identify as an artist. A place to create artwork that allows us to think outside of our military experiences, to use our imagination to write poetry, short stories, science fiction or the hardest of memoirs, to communicate through visual images, to heal through the articulation of our collective voices.

Warrior Writers is a place for us to find community, support and the opportunity to explore creative expression whether it be writing, photography, paper-making, drawing, etc. It is an organization that seeks to share the varied and textured experiences of veterans, where we can relate to each other's experiences and feel a sense of understanding. The community has empowered us to speak honestly about our experiences in the military and the transition to civilian life. While these experiences can be difficult, the silence that we are expected to keep is more dangerous than the harsh words we may share.

Attending a workshop or event can be quite daunting; for some veterans, the thought of talking about military experiences makes them nervous. But after the initial fear, most veterans feel grateful to be in a space where people understand their experiences, accept them and offer support. We invite you to give it a chance.

Warrior Writers is not only about the production of art. It is more about the belief that we can utilize creativity and a creative community to move forward in our lives through workshops, retreats, performances, exhibits and other creative ventures.

Warrior Writers is a Philadelphia-based, national organization whose mission is to create a culture that articulates veterans' experiences, provides a creative community for artistic expression, and bears witness to the lived experiences of warriors. We serve veterans and active duty soldiers of the U.S. military, but focus primarily on those who have served since 9/11.

We host writing workshops, art exhibitions and retreats where veterans come together in group sessions to create works that address their experiences. These workshops have been held all around the country including: Philadelphia, New York City, Chicago, Boston, Colorado, Missouri, Baltimore, Savannah and near Fort Hood, Texas. As a result of our workshops, we have published two anthologies of veterans' written and visual work, *Move, Shoot and Communicate* (2007) and *Re-Making Sense* (2008). See our website to order them, www.warriorwriters.org.

Warrior Writers after a performance in Denver, Colorado, 2010.

HOLLYWOOD / ERIC ESTENZO

EDITOR'S NOTES

LOVELLA CALICA, FOUNDING DIRECTOR

this is not the voice of a veteran
it is the varied voices
the treasured texture
the brutal honesty
the memories
stories to tell
things to forget
the juxtaposition
of ourselves upon ourselves

varied voices

What you have in your hand is a powerful collection of art that makes its mark in the world, that stomps its foot through this book so as not to be hidden or forgotten, that speaks honestly to shed light on some of the issues that veterans face on a daily basis.

This book showcases a broad range of veterans—from those who don't identify as artists, to those who have built their lives around it, to those who make it part of their daily lives in unique ways, to those who are uncovering their creative selves.

This book is proof that no veteran is the same. You may never again think of a veteran as a carbon copy of all the others, but in the myriad of ways that they present themselves here. We cannot deny anyone's experience, but remember that there is more than one reality, that many different things can be true at once.

as you scan the sections

The art in the following pages will grab hold of your emotions, may infuriate you, confuse you, may scald you. This work is not painless. But I ask you, do not turn away from these voices of our veterans.

It is up to all of us to hear our history, to refuse to disregard the voices of veterans and to utilize this creative expression as a bridge to move forward together. These stories must be heard, they must be taken into our lives, into our plans, our communities, into our consciousness to help create a map towards our collective future.

This art is inside them, they shall not hide it and will not deny it. It documents moments in their lives; however harsh or temporary, it is still true and real. So I ask you to struggle with them, with yourself, with the truth. It is not comfortable work, but it is critical.

There are veterans in our communities who need this book, who need this creative veteran community to be able to find the support to move forward, to grow, to come home…please help them find us. Show them that there are veterans that they can relate to, who will walk the road beside them. This book contains the artwork of more than sixty veterans, but that is little compared to the number of veterans in this country who can benefit from artistic exploration and connecting with other veterans.

We know you are out there, and we're here for you. Come forth, sit at the table with us and write yourself alive, write to connect yourselves to one another, to a new lineage, a literary history, the creative construction of a way forward.

from my eyes

Upon publication of our last book in 2008, we had completed only five workshops, and now we've hosted more than eighty workshops around the country.

It has been a blessing to me to watch their artistic efforts to process events and feelings, to survive through this with ink and character, creating with lens, hands and paper a testimony of strength; it is possible, it is cathartic, it is nourishing.

For many of the veterans featured in this book, the days of wearing their uniform under the hot desert sun is many years behind them. Yet still it sits with them. Still the war is not shaken from their skin. They wear it everyday.

I do not nothing but
I do nothing but stand beside
I do nothing but look forward
I do nothing but hear you
I do nothing but remember what I cannot remember
I am grateful for your lives
I am grateful for your voices
for your moving on
for your outpouring of words and sounds and images to build your road forward
it is with these words you walk
it is with our willingness to absorb them
that we remain
that we create
that we sustain
that we can rebuild

FOREWORD
BRIAN TURNER

As I write this, up to 45,000 US troops in Iraq scramble to pack their duffle bags and rucksacks and load up their gear before returning to America. The mission in Afghanistan appears to be far from over, and yet politicians speak of security handovers and the NATO mission there drawing down by the year 2014. With tens of thousands of troops coming home and so many others operating in countries all over the globe, the publication of this anthology carries a certain prescience: the voices gathered in this anthology, in aggregate, seem to suggest that we would be wise to take stock of where we are now, as a country.

That said—I hesitate to travel further in this line of thinking. I don't want to assume the soapbox, the lectern, the high ground of wisdom. While the voices in this volume speak eloquently to the events of our time, they are also far more complicated and nuanced than that stock phrase is capable of conveying. As a student of history, I often gripe about the plethora of historical accounts written from a bird's-eye-view—histories which follow the gestures and actions of the powerful and famous, of kings and queens, of generals and tyrants, of those in high places who issue orders to concentrations of troops positioned on two-dimensional maps laid out before them. I'd rather hear what it was like for the grunt, for the sailor, for the airman, for the marine. I'd rather hear about the human being who had to survive far beyond the privileged air of war's abstract lexicon.

Here is a poem I wrote in 2004 while serving as an infantry sergeant in Iraq with the 2nd Infantry Division, a poem that warns, through the use of sand in its relentless burial, about the dangers of forgetting:

To Sand
To sand go tracers and ball ammunition.
To sand the green smoke goes.
Each finned mortar, spinning in light.
Each star cluster, bursting above.
To sand go the skeletons of war, year by year.
To sand go the reticles of the brain,
the minarets and steeple bells, brackish
sludge from the open sewers, trashfires,
the silent cowbirds resting
on the shoulders of a yak. To sand
each head of cabbage unravels its leaves
the way dreams burn in the oilfires of night.

The imperative to remember is a crucial one. The third Warrior Writer's anthology offers a wide range of voice and experience which functions, in some ways, as an act of witness. An act of memory. It forms a portion of the artistic testament our time calls out into the world. As a bridge spans the difficult crossing, the work in this anthology offers the imagination a place to cross over, a place where experience is not relegated to the erasure of sand.

After more than a decade of news reports, newspaper columns, and stump speeches from politicians articulating the events of our time in language so often removed from the people they are talking about, I encourage you to listen to the voices gathered in this anthology. Page by page, the sand recedes. Page by page, we might better understand the world we live in and the people who live in it.

Brian Turner served in the United States Army for seven years. He deployed to Iraq from 2003 to 2004 as an infantry team leader with the 3rd Stryker Brigade Combat Team, 2nd Infantry Division. He is the author of *Here, Bullet* (2005) and *Phantom Noise* (2010).

INTENTION

LIAM MADDEN

I desire to trust life
to cultivate my unique and needed gifts
Loving with abandon
I intend to weave a web of gratitude into my community

I intend to create a healthy body that gracefully moves me
into sacred relationships with people and places
Living indulgently, feeding
a laughter-appetite an ocean wide

I intend to create a home
filled with friends and magical moments
of connection, fun and creativity
That will become the new routine

I intend to unpave streets and bring sunlight onto bare earth
to grow a city you could mistake for a garden
where working is mistaken for play
Our time abundant for passion and rest

I intend to create a bank of gratitude
an economy of thankfulness
Circulating our sacred gifts
to our deepest needs

I intend to be happy on the journey
Instead of delaying my joy until the destination
experiencing life present and vibrantly alive
in the beautiful world we are creating

"What sticks to memory, often, are those odd little fragments that have no beginning and no end..."

Tim O'Brien, Vietnam Veteran, Author
—from "The Things They Carried"

TALIL AIRBASE

STAY ALERT
STAY ALIVE

"The struggle becomes the very thing that brings us closest to our fellow man and the deep yearning to stay alive, to protect, to suffer, and to endure...together. The struggle becomes nirvana. . . . the greatest lesson of war: our brothers on the battlefield are everything, and all else, including our own lives, is nothing."

Tyler Boudreau, Iraq Veteran, Author
— from "Packing Inferno: The Unmaking of a Marine"

TURNTABLES
NATHAN LEWIS

If things were the other way around

20-year-old Iraqi soldiers would write home to girlfriends about the cold New York winter. About watching snow blow from frozen lakes.

A Captain would stand under a tall pine in Appalachia and call home to Baghdad on a satellite phone. He'd try to be cheerful and tell them about skunks, hummingbirds and the mountains.

Children would scribble the number and type of every enemy vehicle in Crayon.

A patrol of foreign mercenaries wiped out. The corpses hung from the Brooklyn Bridge. Youngsters in hoodies and tims laughing it up for the camera.

Graffiti on concrete barriers would tell Iraqis to go home in broken Arabic.

Jon Stewart would throw his shoes at President Maliki.

Elderly home owners behind every door, clutching shotguns, waiting for the house raids. Thousands of Iraqi soldiers would be shipped home in sleek metal containers draped with a corresponding flag.

There would be withdrawal timetables and multi-national water corporations bidding on Lake Erie. There'd be retired Iraqi generals on Al-Jazeera talking about Canada giving advanced weaponry to insurgents. The politicians would tell you all about the need to occupy Texas in order to keep Mexico out.

Iraqi soldiers would take re-enlistment oaths under the St. Louis arch, in the shadow of the Washington Monument. Two hundred thousand protestors march down Haifa Street demanding an end to the war. Iraqi veterans return to mosques, classrooms and Parliament to speak about the murder and destruction. The war crimes.

There would be rebels in the woods called the Yellow Ribbon Brigade. Red Dawn in every town. If things were the other way around, we'd know the unjust sting of occupation.

WOMB OF WoMD

KRISTINA VOGT

The womb of the WoMD.[1]
Training to see
Through mud, arms low crawling.
In the womb of the WoMD.
Training to hear
The sirens, a call to yonder
Gunshots from where?
In the womb of WoMD.
Training to feel
The body or bag,
To dress right.
In the womb in the WoMD.
Training to know
Approximately killing, approximately enemies
Within the approximate
Reality of the womb of the WoMD.

A proximal reality.
Within the parameters of motive, equidistant to humanity, proportionate to
ability, at level with respect, parallel to resilience, in common to the whole,
divisible by truth
That the womb gives birth
To the WoMD.

---

[1] Weapons of Mass Destruction

A JAZZ REQUIEM FOR THE MALE OF THE SPECIES

JEFF KEY

(to be read aloud with Miles Davis' "Shh, Peaceful")

What you have offered me is bleak
And white
And sterile
And cold.
Marked only by the black scars of industry,
Slavery and greed.
What is offered now to me, the male of the species?

What have you presented to me
As my options,
As my life?
What lie have you believed
And passed on to me
As my possibility?

What have you led me,
A small child and trusting
To believe was my highest hope
And dignity?

What have you denied me in the way of acceptance
And community?
What bleak and barren, white sky, raped mountains and choking factory
Phallus,
What hopeless and hollow aspiration is mine to bear
Because I am man?

Is a man worth no more than his labor?
Is a man worth no more than his sweat?
Is a man worth no more than his blood?

My father's boots lie discarded and work-worn
As his black-lung'd body.
My grandfather's boots lie caked with dried blood and the
Soil of distant lands he lacked the education to know of before he went there,
Sent on the big grey and grim coffin afloat,

Draped in the American flag.
And his father before him
And his before him.

What will you now offer me as a man?
Am I not worth more than the blood and happiness I will shed in battle?
For promised liberty then withheld?
For fake freedom and rumors of democracy?
Or more likely for those who withhold
From we who fight
The spoils of empire?
For the black oily secret
Best left buried
That now flows uninhibited
Into the warm gulf of Mother's sweet emotion?

What will you offer a man like me?
A man who is willing to celebrate you,
A man who is more like you than you care to believe?

The fateful waiter
Stands at my table
With offers of callousness
And of putrid meat
When all I desire is Love.

What now have you afforded me,
A man born of a woman
And the injury done her by another man
Damaged, himself by same lack of understanding,
Of choices?
Real. Choices.

Why must you hate me because you've been hurt?
I am hurt too!
Why must you hate me because of my
Anatomy?

Look at me, I beg you
Are you certain I am the monster you fear?
I share your desire of a man's body!
I share your hunger for peace,
And I am more like you than you think.
I am more like you than you think.

Does that spoil your worldview?
I cannot,
Will not

Apologize.

Why because of some hateful heritage committed by those who preceded me,
Male and female
Have you have robbed me of my greatest hope
And all the beauty of my unfulfilled potential?

Dragged from the warmth, comfort and anxiety of my mother's body
I am thrust into an existence for which I am ill prepared.
The human male is alive outside the womb but seconds
Before the first blow comes,
And then the lifetime sentence,
"It's a boy, it's a boy, it's a boy!"
I am thrust into a world of bright lights, frightening noises, antiseptic
Aggravation and isopropyl expectation.
(Even as I speak these words you withdraw from me any willingness you
might have had to adore me, to welcome and to listen.)
I did not hurt you.
I will not hurt you.
And I do not regret being a man.

In diapers at tender age I am confused to see the compassion my sisters are
Afforded whenever they fall.
Not to wish them deprived as I am but to partake in that delicious form of
Love myself.
"Boys don't cry. Boys don't cry."
I cry.
To look with longing at pretty things
And sensitive colorful and comfortable
And soft
And warm
And happy.
(The acknowledgement of male oppression does not diminish the
acknowledgement of female oppression. It seeks to end it!)

So may I
But for this one time
Speak of the atrocity visited upon me
And upon my brothers
Without offending,
Without drawing fire?

On the white hash-marked and numbered field we are encouraged to "play"
To compete
To win
To "vanquish the enemy"
Poorly disguised versions of myself
On neat facsimiles of future battlefields

In preparation for war.

How long has it been true
That the greatest to which a man can aspire
Is to die in war?

In the somewhat happier tune
A man is worth his ability to work,
To bring home the bacon,
(Even if I do keep kosher and vegan,
And love the beast
And love to run naked with the beast
In the woods beside him
Rather to than kill him.)

I am no killer.

Is this the life you offer me,
To squelch my Divinity?
And dare I say it, my
Femininity.
Take it then if you like,
If those are your terms
Give my body to the worms.

The greatest offense
A boy can do
Is to be considered "like a woman"
How then can you act surprised
When we do
What we do?

I went to war.
I put on the uniform
And went to do
What you told me would make me loved by you.
I stopped myself from loving (or tried)
I stopped my nurturing nature (or tried)
I sought to see the Iraqis as my enemies
As separate from me
But I could not.

My Native blood was too strong.
My compassionate heart too wise,
To believe anything
Other than the Truth.

I am like a woman too,

If only in secret.

If crying for those who suffer,
Is being like a woman, let me be womanly.
Or more likely let me be like a man,
A man as he should be,
A man as Creation intended him to be.

My nature is to be an ally to womankind.
My nature is to champion her.
My nature is to lift her up when she falls
And walk beside her.
How many times in my life have I been met by contempt of a woman
Because she made dreadful assumptions about me?
When she could not see my two-spirited spirit,
When she mistook my form for my intention?

Yes, I have heard you.
Yes, my heart breaks with your suffering,
And yes, I too have been destroyed by the same sick system
Of sexism and misogyny,
Cruelty and ignorance.
Please Mother, welcome me home.

Take back the mask
My face is destroyed by it.
I have sacrificed my soul on the altar of American Masculinity.
Please Mother, welcome me home.

I have watched horrified
As men became boys,
Rattled and ruined
When the game
Became real
And the cost of defeat multiplied.
Please Mother, welcome us home.
Please Sister, welcome us home.

A speck to your eye
In the white blistered sky
Far above the ruins of my iniquity
And the rabble of industry
And the shame of slavery
And the life that you offered me,
I reach for That which created me,
Please Mother, welcome me home.

PARENTS OF WARRIORS
CHERISH HODGE

In my darkest hour, I wonder at times why we have children anymore. Aside from the biological natural processes, aside from the knee-jerk reaction coming from know-it-all inquisitives, I begin to ask this question daily on a spiritual level.

Why do we raise precious eyes, chubby hands, warm skin, soft, thin, wispy hair and golden laughs if we are to raise them to travel their grown but not forgotten beauty onto a path of death and haunted warring? I'm daunted by the shame we face when we sew socks and build coffins... buy backpacks full of school supplies and finance bombs that shatter schools resembling shacks.

What then do I say to my son when he wanders into the sun with a rifle on his back and a bullet mark on his chest? This is beyond saving our way, saving our values or saving our ass. This is sending our barely grown babies to stand within a machine-made storm that doesn't have to exist. Are we powerless when they are tiny and some ill willed condition threatens their unbridled face of innocence? Not for a second.

Then why now mothers and fathers are we powerless while receiving flags upon our laps, situated in front of Our Blood, our barely recognizable, cold, hardened, hidden children who lie silently in a standard issue tomb?

As a mother, as a soldier, as an American, I still cannot find substantial reasoning. I question any parent and their professed unconditional love who indeed can. I am not fighting with the rightful notion that you cannot force your child as an adult to avoid military service or military belief. Parents must delicately encourage their child where they can. But then knowing that your son or daughter is now far away, alone and in the hands of bombed fate, you must rise up and be the soldier your child can lean on. Working to end wars, investing in common ground, forcing governments to promote peace and peaceful relations should become the cornerstone of each day. Because each day, the cornerstone for their child is just trying to survive. It is beyond work, beyond just a job and beyond simply trying to do service — to try and survive something they honestly don't even understand.

THE RECRUITER

CHANTELLE BATEMAN

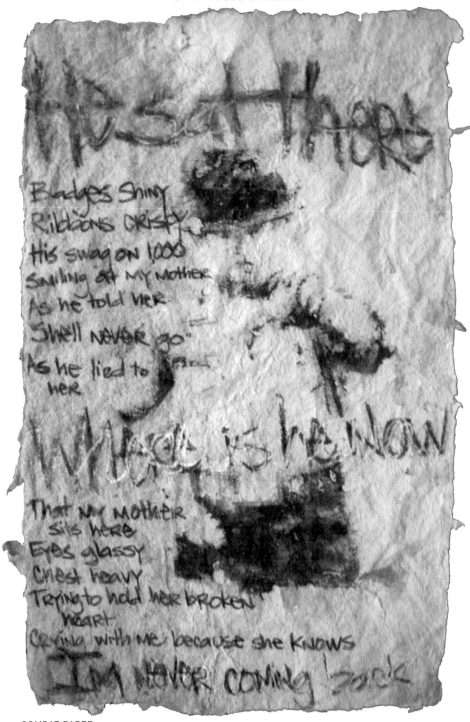

He saw Haters

Badges shiny
Ribbons crispy
His swag on 1,000
Smiling at my mother
As he told her
"She'll never go"
As he lied to
her

Where is he now

That my mother
sits here
Eyes glassy
Chest heavy
Trying to hold her broken
heart
Crying with me because she knows
I'm never coming back

A LETTER TO THE WAR PRESIDENTS

RAYMOND CAMPER

Since my generation was born, nearly every U.S. President oversaw some major military operation in a foreign country, and to date, only two presidents during my generation didn't serve within the military. This is a letter to every U.S. President that has overseen a war, yet had never seen war firsthand.

Would you shed one drop of blood
for the gallons that we've given,
would you last one day in the conditions
we've spent years in?

Would you be able to sign on the dotted line,
and follow the directives sent down from on high
when they went against your convictions of wrong and right?

Would you be able to look your family in the face,
and tell them it was worth it,
when you can't forgive yourself,
for the carnage you partook in?

You have not engaged your enemy at close range,
seen the sweat and fear upon his face,
before you forever erased him away.

My generation has done this and more,
some of us while questioning,
others while adoring,
nonetheless,
we are the children who you will bury,
without ever knowing what our level of sacrifice feels like.

Would you give just one drop of bravery,
for the oceans we've turned red with everything in our veins
to bring an end to the bitter fruits
not even your precious offspring will ever be allowed to taste?

INDOCTRINATION

PETER SULLIVAN

We did jumping jacks until we called them side-straddle hops.
We walked with ruck sacks on our backs until we called it humping.
We fired guns until we called them weapons.
We accepted punishment until we called it discipline.
We shouted for death until we called it singing.
We studied myths until we called them realities.
We shot at plastic people until we called them "enemy."
We trained to oppress populations until we called it liberating them.
We said things about stomping babies until we called them jokes.
We did the wrong things until we called them right.
We lived in fear until we called it courage.
We called it something else until we believed it.

DAYDREAM LEGACY

MAGGIE MARTIN

GI Joe in the box, anticipation building, compressing.
Cami-clad roosters puff chests, but scare like skittish dogs
when thunder cracks.
To all things "brave" and "honorable"
we sacrifice ourselves,
words, oaths, and codes we are dying to believe.
Looming clouds of hubris block out the light,
Then vanish like phantoms in the quiet.
The desert hums.
Caravan of elephants winding to the horizon,
Shaking the ground with excitement.
Fear. Lust for relevance.
I, in this traveling band of actors,
brothers and sisters, strangers, imposters.
Channeling Joan of Arc and Forrest Gump.
Generation who cares?
I was looking for something more, than reality TV.
A chance at redemption.

WHO'S THE ENEMY?

JACOB GEORGE

this is for my battle buddy, Cooper, who in basic training
lay on the floor in a pool of his own blood
teeth missing, eyes swollen shut
I could see the boot prints on his face
beat for bein' black, beat for his race
this is for G-force
the brick house jumpmaster, paratroopin' disaster
Maaan, he could sing!
and make everyone laugh
but they called him names when he turned his back
see, G took care of me and I trusted him for that
he taught me how to fly, how to pull the trigger
and no Afghani ever called him nigger

this is for the Vietnam Vet
who told me he didn't fear the death he might meet
because of his skin color,
he already worried about bein' strung up
just for walkin' down his own street

we were told the military would teach us
how to share our freedom
but what we learned was a new level of hate

when we weren't training to kill people with turbans
we were conditioned to hate our sisters and brothers
foreign, domestic, and urban

this institution thrives on hate

there was a swastika brand on the chest
of my first army roommate
he told me uncle Sam don't care
but I couldn't help but stare

at the absurdity of a man
wearing an arrowhead patch
representing the spirit of the Native Americans
crowned with a U.S. flag, on a blouse
encasing a chest
branded with a symbol of hate
this uniform supposedly defeated?

I've got news for you America
the enemy isn't in the Middle East
or Africa or Asia or Central and South America

It's within you
and it's within me
It's the institution of hate
that keeps people from bein' free

AMERICAN SOLDIER

MICHAEL ANTHONY

Inspired by a Carol Wimmer poem

When I say... I am an American Soldier
I'm not shouting I'm better than you,
I'm whispering, I was a boy, and now find myself a man.

When I say... I am an American Soldier
I speak not only of this with pride
I'm also confessing that I stumble, make mistakes,
And need competent leadership to help guide me,
So I in turn, can be a competent leader.

When I say... I am an American Soldier
I'm not trying to be strong,
I'm professing that I am weak
And need the strength of my peers and country,
To help carry me on.

When I say... I am an American Soldier
I'm not bragging of past successes
I'm admitting I have failed in the past
Admitted the mistakes, and tried to right the wrongs.

When I say... I am an American Soldier
I'm not claiming to be perfect,
My flaws are far too visible
But my country needs me, and I soldier on.

When I say... I am an American Soldier
I can still feel the sting of pain,
From seeing those that I care about die,
While we fight for those that we love.
I have my share of heartaches,
So I call upon the American people,
To help guide our soldiers, when home.

When I say... I am an American Soldier
I'm not saying anything,
I'm just a simple man,
Who was called upon by his country...
To fight.

DEDICATION
TOBY HARTBARGER

Dedication is a brown stain
on the back of your PT[1] shorts
moving down your thighs
one mile no sweat, two miles oh shit
Dedication is a foul scent
in your only pair of running shoes
damn, it's in your insoles
three miles give it hell, four miles might as well
Dedication is a mother fucker
never will the jokes end
shitted on the spirit run

---

[1] Physical Training

THE ESCAPIST

STEVE YOCZIK

BOOMBOOMBOOM

Door crash rattle
Heart explodes
Hands quake
NCO[1] screams
Are you in there?
I don't answer

I hide, evade, escape.
Fear only surpassed by emptiness
helpless
trapped
motivated
resisting

Door unlocks
sergeants enter
I am in my locker
hear the footsteps
snickering,
Huh-huh, maybe he's hiding in the locker
but they never check

they leave, I slither out,
victorious

4 am
PT formation, roll call
I answer here, Sergeant
then step back
walk confidently toward barracks

1st SGT[2] screams
Who the fuck is that? Go check it out
Hey, you in Alpha Company?
NO, I bellow over my shoulder
continue walking, unhindered

Another 4 am Formation
Step back as before
begin walking
hit the tree line
I hide, evade, escape

crawling through the weeds
knowing this place so well

Found:
Yoczik what happened to you??
Sorry Sar'n, I had to take a dump
Never in my life have I ever...
Roger Sar'n, won't happen again...

But it does, over and over and over and over

Suicide night:
Body quakes / heart explodes again
muscles ache from convulsions
memory spotty
Friend watches over me
Fearful denial for 911 call

Eisenhower Army Medical Center
Tubes, catheter, heart monitor
angry NCO who had better things to do

A Lieutenant calls me a liar
Coward
I am inches from his face,
I DID NOT LIE, SIR
I walk away, still alive
STILL ALIVE, FUCK

My friend calls me from Canada:
The First True Soldier I've seen
during this whole fucking nightmare
calling from Canada
Is it possible
Do I have the option
Can I do it

I prepare:
Clothes, cold-weather gear, valuables
Purchase bus ticket on base
Lady gives weird look
Toronto, Canada?
Yes Ma'am
Slide debit card, done and done

Day of departure:
Cold sweat, shaky knees, glancing everywhere
Terrified
Load gear
sink into seat

Low profile
observant, vigilant, determined, scared shitless

Bus takes off
Atlanta
Detroit
Border:
just visiting friends
OK, you have one week to leave
Sounds good, thanks

Three years.
Empty apartment, empty chest, empty attempts
at being friends
Desolate heart
Cold
So fucking cold

BOOMBOOMBOOM

TORONTO PD, PLEASE OPEN THE DOOR SIR
Hand on knife, eyes on door, lights stay off
SIR, PLEASE OPEN THE DOOR
I don't answer
crouched
heart explodes once again
SORRY SIR, WE HAVE THE WRONG ADDRESS

Sigh like my dying breath,
collapse

Time melts, my mind melts, relationships melt away

Government could give a shit
citizens even less
relatives the absolute least

6 years of military
17 years of military upbringing
For what
FOR FUCKING WHAT

An open mind
A free spirit
A will that cannot be broken, no matter how hard you smash the door

---

[1] Non-Commissioned Officer
[2] First Sergeant

CAMI FLAG / LARS EKSTROM

BULLET FLAG / LARS EKSTROM

COMMUNIQUÉ

CHARLIE PALUMBO

My emotional response to a posting by a conscientious objector

Deserted—
Lexicon unbecoming of a leader;
But I am a leader
Becoming deserted.

Compassion, the inability I see in them;
There is no move towards empathy.
Self-aware I couldn't call them;
Unaware I would say to them.

Alpha, top, leader, bottom,
Company,
Mixed,
Commander,
Deafening.

The fear irreversible,
I am conscientious;
I am an objector.

They are my objector,
My captor,
Caging me, enraging me.
Do they listen?

Leaders listen, BUT—
They, they ignore me,
Often, often, my voice is left unheard.

Regulations, I follow them;
I fail all your tests;
They ignore the failure.

They ignore my voice as it grows louder,
Paperwork pushed aside,
Iron fist, ruling tide.

I am leaving now on my own.
I did what was asked;
I did it right.
I am not going to fight that fight.

My choice, my war, my wage,
I am freeing myself out of my head,
Out of their cage.

Did you think I was stupid?

My voice, My pain,
My hurt, My gain,
Leaving this all to stay sane.

TRANSFORMING

SEAN CASEY

You call him son,
You call him hero.

To him he's neither,
Your son is not of the old mold, but an altered, unfamiliar one.

You call him son,
You call him hero.
You cheer and praise his deeds, like parents clapping to an infant to rouse a
cheerful reaction from it.
The parades and waving flags comfort you.

A celebration of his violent profession unnerves him.
He understands now, by his time in the desert, that if they knew the true
story of his profession, they'd be more reserved.

They call him precious,
They reward his sacrifice.
His medals validate his accomplishments in your eyes.
The glittering, clanging dance on his chest calms them, like a lullaby to a toddler.

He remains restless, for vanity can't and shouldn't thrive,
When something has been birthed from the ugliest of circumstances.

UNTITLED
SERGIO KOCHERGIN

A YEAR OF SECRETS

IRIS M. FELICIANO

January 3, 2002
We board an aircraft en route to a secret airbase
with secret boxes with locks and secret codes
We consent

March 8, 2002
We transmit secret signals about enemies
and their secret hideaways for boots to storm
We certify

June 22, 2002
We find a secret stash of hash
and smoke beneath a rock
We approve

July 12, 2002
I am forced into a secret place
and robbed of my greatest secret
ordered never to tell
I succumb

September 4, 2002
We pack up secret photos of boys and girls
of dead camels and burnt homes
We lock them in a secret box with a secret code
We concede

November 17, 2002
We have secret meetings about
how to keep the secrets we were told
We board an aircraft with more secrets than any
box could hold
We assent

December 7, 2002
My love kisses me
Once again we lay in our secret place
together, yet still so alone
We don't share any more secrets
We defer

FREEDOM
DREW CAMERON

COMBAT PAPER

WAR PORN 5: TOTAL WAR

ROY SCRANTON

war is war is war is war. war hell war. war. war is poppies horse

blue skies over black seas, wine-dark life over life over life under death. Nay, we used not to call upon IED[1] attacks and suicide bombs,

young

exulted in thought

documents detailing Tahrir district, gates of hell to abide therein, torture and pass along main supply

Allah true.

So think of the Department of artillery, tank rounds and die, city to kill, employed to carry out the strike. The occupations fight

special officers definitely better than we

gulf with significant success

foot more than 12 hours. "But I think massive aerial strikes that many here said before pilots aboard the USS killed last week ahead for Iraq's interim also went at Mustansiriya University or the senior Library at Basra and Command Council issues wrote about the case of an Iraqi man who—"

world war. world of war. worlds of two we war word war. story war. world war four. word war hell my war cold war   one war two war red war blue war and deadliest whore in the history of human word war six history begins with ends   word history ends internet evolving project   war twelve at twelve a conservative estimate President sworn statement, after his release, thousands of manuscripts and attack in Madrid

again the same, certainly we send apostles by the bench in water and urine

dull rumbling in my ears

tingling command of Allah

we're lost. This statement has Iraq's major museums and libraries for retribution and that time is despite detainees, *The Washington Post*, while cuneiform temporary storage information rehousing two Apache Helicopters recorded en masse National Library over parts of the embattled city seeming Babylonian temple, Academy troops in a Bradley Fighting Vehicle fired the Awqaf city blasts heard empty and all the shops closed for resentments and breed that door, in with all their cunning courage the view that procedures "violated established interrogation" further, performed, sent their genesis not in Iraq but in interrogation care and multiple operations, he did not—ultimately in decisions made unsurvivable in previous wars. The cost, General Fay writes in a section of his report, that the knee, the other in a hip disarticulation will I now burn; it is of no use to you, of how to know if they are true or false, is "have respect shown you by the Trojans," true information, they would have to be different amid her tears, and the women joined virtual as the war itself, and for this reason the virtual violence of consensus, the violence of the   war war   war on the one hand, half a dirty dozen on the other war mine and war dress redress the highest exaltation of masculine glory war good tv   war great tv   sweet song and agony   never war   in addition, due to the Bradley Fighting Vehicles material assets oh yeah, she's bomb, Captain Travis Van Hector first empires, developed window pane man the room. "We're hit," the voice and angle measurement with his eyes while his grenades kill two soldiers, including second millennium BCE[2] which he ate and donated today far beyond the bits I left uptown, 29, of Lomira, Wisconsin. 'Babylonian' mathematics jump the gun, groups of insurgents took over common the wooden mountain of Placus and should be allowed in. End of fucking where they killed seven, a child — ill-starred sire of an ill-starred care many push-ups can you do from the ambush into the house of Hades when we need you to kill somebody, a sorrowing widow in your house. The ancient culture and kill them. As yet a mere infant.

Now that you are, kill.

The first days after the war. Even though he escaped the intense, the action began at 5, his life henceforth one of labor and killing two GIs[3] and wounding mellow, spaced out from waiting, says the sheik the police killed the motorist down the road. He rammed the British. All were driven out

coalition forces prisoners scooped up this way flooded the keepers, harsh terrain, these nighttime sweeps gave 48 hours to campaign on detainees. just war happening. just war theory. but one of them would make war rather than let the nation survive and the other would accept war rather than let it perish, and the war came. It seems an unlikely story — when the resistance inside Iraq now speeding and a soldier got scared, foreign fighters, Saudis or Syrians, he was out to pass. I walk back for Abu Talat; the Qaeda is running the rebellion and 100 percent lunch served captain, headed for sporadic firefights deeper still in Baquba's narrow side streets and relatively insecure government Abu taken at random; many more report "broken systems" and the cuneiform tablet collection honor itself, besieged, sweltering, stinking US marine guards monument interpreters, interrogators, detainees team's efforts, he could not be revived. Including edible food, and that, at its height before Iraq's interim government to gain radio of seventy-five to one, the fighters launched a series of coordinated Ricardo Sanchez, which lacked among targets Baghdad, Mosul, Ramadi and Baquba (Full story): the united states urged iraq to adopt a new hydrocarbon law that would enable us and other foreign companies to news analysis comment interactive on the course and impact of detailed historical information map conflicts, especially those from the first photographs links articles biographical boyfriend came back from the war. after dinner they left us alone. in-depth oral history and analysis of the war based on interviews with political leaders between the sexes in punic gulf frontier any civil. These shall enter the garden resistance and US forces killed at least Bush's ultimatum
    light of his sky

        another in the fire, then the secret one read by Jordan, a lot of pressure to produce and other interrogation centers O my people! how is it that I, here in Baquba, a small UN that I should disbelieve in early

morning attacks by resistance fighters with knowledge and *I call you to occupy the building*. He saw the truth and said no title to be called to, Abdel Humam who lives downtown I deemed that hero Deiphobus the extravagant everything and kicked the Americans out; death is not indeed exceeding chief of Diyala Province, told al-Jazeera TV for so Jove and his son Apollo the far-darter have
under control

later, resistance fighters set 21 Iraqi police today, beheaded, said they are collaborators with the greatest affair of state, the basis of life and death the
tao of survival or extinction thoroughly pondered and
analyzed war man   war language   war metaphor   rocks and stones and horses   war songs on the horizon   war rifles and knives   blood and steel   war propaganda dogs see war run run war run seen war   never war   seen war all the war a strategy of weakness. By late summer pointed to the breast which had suckled him. Officials expected to start drawing down Hector, my son, spurn not this breast, but occupation force of no more than 30,000 Americans comfort from my own bosom, 130,000
troops, loosing the initiative to protect us from this man; stand not nowhere and, after carrying out its increasingly managed disappear, intelligence officers kill me as easily as though there is no parleying with him for some rock
incidence of penetrating wounds. Better fight him at once, gunshot wounds, shrapnel injuries or blast thus did he stand and ponder, but Achilles is required far more frequently than in civilian   taking up, I begin to
feel

of holes

a blacktop guided in a bad hundred feet down Gulf added to the brass
shell dogs devour battle so they too
no from previous wars

each knows i have seen seen what seen war seen war seen it seen tv war the tv seen war war yes war on tv   what seen seen felt sand sweat yes
war on tv   seen war   yes tv war we are we war   bewar came down to war upon the war, and many wars had to war against war for a long, long war the war all war
war all the war never war seen war

Improvised Explosive Device
[2] Before Common Era
[3] General Issue

GREED WALKS
ERIC ESTENZO

KA-KA-KALLISTI

TOM AIKENS

Scotty! Scotty you whisper and stutter —
you remember — kallisti[1] — you dyin' man.

It's the ch-ch-chatter that scattered those ghosts — that battered rabble
baptized in ashes, shattered that apple Scotty, Scotty the worms
are in your eyes —
you dyin' man.

Momma, momma, momma, She said ka-ka-kallisti!
Ain't no Yahweh[2] — Scotty cries while
parents are at home, at home and Scotty,
Scotty's all alone, poor poor Scotty,
only hearin' a god he don't believe in — She's smilin' now —
someone Scotty,
someone knows.
Scotty, you dyin'.

I know Scotty, I was there too
with the g-g-ghosts in the ruins, that rocked rocky road, the explosion
where the apple plunked you bled,
Scotty — eyes, ears and She knows.
She chose you, saw you and you?
You dyin' man.

Her voice crows hoarse
hun-gar-ree
and that metre measured your moments left,
timbre and pitch — down.
Yeah Scotty, you know.
You know you dyin'.

It was that second — that pause-those paws-those claws clipped your ride.
Sand rained!...the sound — it — made —
the eyes, Her eyes, watched you Scotty,
they know-they know-they know-they know they
know you dyin' man.

So Scotty when Yahweh laughs, turn
that other cheek and smile. That apple,
that apple was yours, you were —
kinda still are — the best of us.
We miss you, and we're w-w-waiting.

---

[1] the word ΚΑΛΛΙΣΤΗΙ (Ancient Greek: καλλίστη(ι) kallistē(i), Modern Greek: καλλίστη kallisti;
"for / to the most beautiful") [4] was inscribed on the Golden Apple of Discord by Eris (cont. on page 42)
[2] the name of God in the Bible; the word Yahweh is a modern scholarly convention for the Hebrew יהוה,
transcribed into Roman letters as YHWH and known as the Tetragrammaton.

WOMEN'S WORK

JOYCE WAGNER

CLOSE UP PHOTO OF LARGER WORK

Joyce Wagner created "Women's Work" in her kitchen using a blender to pulp recycled domestic advertisements (junk mail) with spices and flour. She assembled the paper/collage on a large window screen. It contains images of her own ultrasound and photocopies and etchings from photos of her experience in Iraq.

THIS WORLD

JASON ROBERT MIZULA

This world is a broken place I'm sure of it
but the rest of my life I shall spend on the mending path
a lost soul soldier of this human race
keeping pace with the forces of dark and destructive hearts
who look out for just number one not one love
as I wish every man would do how about you?
Will you just sit back and watch the unraveling
nation versus nation father versus son
some say the world's ending but we've only begun
I know there's some goodness in everyone's heart
some choose to ignore it and push us apart
but we all bleed the same blood
we breath the same air sing the same sad songs
and know it's not fair when one man dies of hunger
some throw away food we turn off CNN
when it sours our mood.
But the channels don't matter who needs a TV
when it doesn't concern us what our eyes don't see.
Some eyes don't see homelessness and despair
but beyond the white picket fence it's still there.
Mogadishu to Gaza
Port-au-Prince to Baghdad
and hell south of the border
we think we've got it bad?
Tsunamis and famine malaria, aids
and death and destruction in the wake of air raids.
This world's not an Xbox and war's not a game
some good people die on both sides just the same.
Fathers and daughters
mothers and sons
and when it's all over just who's really won?
"Whatsoever you do to the least of my people"
are the words that we hear from beneath the steeple
yet some choose to shun those who differ in kind
for their sake I hope that their savior is blind.
To kill is to kill to steal is to steal
no matter the guise or the noble appeal.

FT. HOOD WAITING

AARON HUGHES

Evictions
Cigarettes
Fast food
Painkillers
Tranquilizers
Sleeping pills
Dreams
Uniforms
Red eyes
Sunrise
Paper work
Waiting
Standing
Waiting

Sunset
Cigarettes
Soda pop
Leaving
Coming
Sweat
Memorials
Sweaty palms
Dead grass
Flags
Identification
Death
Waiting
Cigarettes butts
Waiting

Time

WOUNDED AND WAITING

NICK MORGAN

Fill the room with chatter.
Hold silence in a box.
Not one shaped like a heart
but one forged in my mind
and secured by self preservation.
Waste not your essential liberties
on egregious erosions of mind.
Fuck pseudo-safety at freedom's cost.

Unchecked aggression is stripped away
and churned into betrayed confusion.
Confessions of honesty hopelessly deprived,
smothered by coals heating irate flames.
No shame or apologies from turned cheeks.
Waning when the sky turns gray.
Cracking like thunder in moments alone.
They have me in fatal check,
wounded and waiting in fear.

I am staring into the near distance
like an aged man of burden.
Is this how it is forever going to be?
The weeks go on as days die,
and I cannot look in the mirror
at this ever changing profile.

Instead, I divert my gaze to
a man standing awkwardly on the corner.
Tormented in his head.
Screaming at every flash and bang.
Never calm.
Seeking diversion…
His death was long ago.

EVISCERATED

ROBYNN MURRAY

I am your walking wounded broken toy soldier,
and your flag is burning and all your yellow ribbons have fallen down.
I cut open these festers to force your eyes to see the truth so damn it, LOOK!
Look at what has become of me, of us.

I will gladly reopen these wounds if there is change that will come of it.
So that no one else receives these scars.

We walking wounded broken toy soldiers
salute your burning flags, untie your yellow ribbons
and bind up our open wounds that are proudly on display for you.

But most bow your heads low,
and shut tightly your eyes
ignoring our evisceration.

ROBYNN'S STORIES / LOVELLA CALICA

PLASTIC ARMY MAN

TYLER ZABEL

i'm not your plastic army man
i'm not your toy to play with in the sand
you don't own me or my soul
i've broken free to grow and be whole

i'm not your government issue
or a broken weapon to be misused
i am my own man and i don't need your game
this lion's still got teeth and he will not be tamed

take your bullets and your guns, i don't need 'em to feel safe
i'm not gonna turn and run, i don't need to duck and strafe
take your rage and fury, i don't need it anymore
i've forgotten what i ever thought i would've used it for

now i am before you, here to make my final stand
your fear cannot control me, i am not in your command
not in your command
not in your command
I   Am   NOT   in   your   command

Tyler Zabel performs at the Intrusive Thoughts show,
National Veterans Art Museum, Veterans Day 2010.

THE PART OF OURSELVES WE'RE AFRAID OF

VICTOR INZUNZA

I found the devil in a fist,
in the shadows
of the part of ourselves we're afraid of,
in a shadow we belong to.

He hides in whispered lies that taunt our lonely eardrums,
in roads that lead to strange tongues.

He hides in the twitches on the tips of fingers
that dance
on the outskirts of a trigger.

He hides where the haze and the gunfire swell the fear
of the things that starve for blood.

He hides in a paranoid flicker on the horizon,
as the moonlight stains our skin,
and the visions of night reflect on our
sleep-deprived eyes.
We get an artillery shell symphony for a lullaby
and a nightmare for a good night's rest.

There's a price tag on my M-16.
There's a price tag on our lives.
There's a price tag on every breath.

Our chests are an Arlington graveyard,
where we bury the dead thing beneath the skin.

JOHN JARED

DAN CONERD

December 4th 2008 a day I will never forget
December 4th 2008 a day that is forever stained and burned in my mind
December 4th 2008 my phone rang in the early morning
December 4th 2008 I was told that my best friend was dead

With only 4 days left in his deployment
With only 4 days left til he was home
With only 4 days left til he would be back drinking a beer
With only 4 days left til he would be planning his drive to Denver, Colorado

It wasn't suppose to be like this
It wasn't suppose to happen to him
It wasn't suppose to be this hard
It wasn't suppose to end

He was a friend
He was a brother
He was a son
He was a father

In death his name will live on
In death his legacy will continue
In death his stories will be told
In death his memory will remain

I miss his motivation
I miss his words of wisdom
I miss his ability to live life
I miss his presence

Everyday I think about the times in Germany
Everyday I think about the times in Iraq
Everyday I think about it should have been me and not him
Everyday I think about WHY

Iraq, For the Oil?
Iraq, for the money?
Iraq, for the sense of adventure?
Iraq, for the protection of the country?

John Jared Savage was a comedian
John Jared Savage was a loyal friend
John Jared Savage was a great man
John Jared Savage will always be remembered!!

SHE'S STILL HERE WITH ME

SARAH LASALLA BOOKER

(for Jeannette)

I remember:
dark storms rolling behind eyes
brimming with humor
flooded with confidence
and spilling compassion beyond its boundaries.

I.

You asked me
"Who the hell are you?"
on my first day
but you didn't say hell
and I didn't have any answers.

II.

You loved them and told me so
each story progressively painting
a picture in my mind
your brother the Marine, your proud father,
your mother, who left long before you did,
patiently waiting on the other side.

III.

Home grew into a long stretch of shoreline
refuge and respite
except you'd never been
until one summer when we went together

Red swimsuit and churning sea
initiating peals of laughter
you looked so funny
turning your back on the waves.

IV.

Summer moving too quickly
between our fingers slipping
away like dreams
into the empty blue sky

clinging warm to our brown skin
with words and promises
of correspondence and telephone calls
but never rematerializing
the way it was.

Bahama-Mama's before you caught a flight
to become a California girl.
Only a few months later
you urged me to come see you
at the barracks
when you stopped over
before Kandahar.

V.

The phone still sits trapped,
caught in the web of memory
your voice hanging in the air
weaves between my ears.

VI.

I have tried to change my mind
to take back my youthful immortality
and follow your voice.

It floats away
to the wind
to the Mountain
and I can't find it anymore.

VII.

I saw your face
on someone else
and I must have looked shocked.
It wasn't you, but I stared anyway
until she wouldn't walk by me anymore.
She didn't know
I was just looking through shadows.

THE DEAD MOVE ON

TOM AIKENS

Smoking in silence by a quiet tomb;
each drag briefly lights the inscription. I
stand by a grave in the snow. Flakes flash in
descent. Smoke trails loosely in the wind, as

I see, in brief reflections, the newly
dead walking on stone, their deeds wrapped in ribbon.
An American flag withers by the grave,
left by a widow who had once

wrapped herself as a veiled, black, leaking stain
across his flag-sheathed mahogany frame—
who had once crawled into his open grave
after him. I watched and cried "No, Lena"

and dreamed him alive and laughing at me.
The cold seeps in, and the snow swirls around
in that grave silence that scores guilt,
or sorrow, reflection coming in flashes.

LYNN ESTOMIN

*"Lips parched with fatigue
taste like earth and crack like rock,
breath hangs aching in burned lungs
too scorched to exhale."*

Sarah LaSalla Booker, Afghanistan Veteran, Warrior Writer
—from "Masirah"

CAMEL HERDER

WALKING UPON THE HOLY LAND

"... never seen such compassion: the hands

of the medic as he ran gentle
fingers through the boy's hair: 'it's going to

be alright ...'"

Tom Aikens, Iraq Veteran, Warrior Writer
—from "Responsibility"

ANOTHER DAY AT THE OFFICE

AMY HERRERA

the phone rings and I answer
I hear a crackled voice coming from a radio
this time it's a fighter somewhere over Baghdad
I swivel in my chair, and turn down the CNN program I was watching
I brief him on three locations in and around the city
like call of duty, the mission unfolds before me on the computer screen
if it's not live, it's not real,
or so you hope
it's the last brief of my shift, and I'm ready to go home
he has been engaged for most of the day in country
we have both had a long day and are ready to rest
while I get into my car and he lands his plane, I wonder,
"How many did we kill today?"

ITSY BIG ASS SPIDER

CHANTELLE BATEMAN

Big, Hairy, and Scary
They have hidden weapons
So we get to them first
Before their big, hairy, scary arms could touch me
Before they could overtake us at night

They said
"Watch out for them!"
In big meetings
With big people
We talked about the big, hairy, scary things
They aren't nice
Not pets, not friends
We collected them in jars anyway
Prodded them in their glass prisons
Shook them up, down, and around

Big, hairy, and scary
DON'T LET THEM OUT!
They'll be angry
They'll come for you
I stayed vigilant
Boot ready to strike
No big hairy scaries would come for me

I never saw one
Not a single big hairy scary
Only the jarred trophies of boys
With too much anger and free time
Tiny, hairy, and scared

THE CONCRETE ABYSS

FRED LAMBERT

During the burning day, dusty boots and straining sinews ram through the hinges.
I enter, up front, inserting my rifle into the crushed avenue first.
My rifle is wet. She's ready for fun.
I follow her, trusting her urges and powers.
She charms me forward to flirt with others, black like a widow.
Back and forth goes her nose, a sneaking proboscis with venom,
searching dark chasms for the inevitable.
It never comes, and the thrill is gone. Another dry hole.

Past dusk I see him again.
Stumbling forward under eastern fabrics, my eyes avert.
Earlier, while the sun oppressed,
the flies planted their spawn as I observed.
Dotted like black legions,
they twitched on his beard and rotten, mask-like features,
working their way to his brain,
which lay like a display specimen neatly nearby.
The other grunts snapped flashes like tourists, and I joined in, too.
Now we are alone in the street.

A white star pops; it's followed by a flood of amber light and dancing shadows,
bringing adolescent gooseflesh to rise,
with childlike visions of lurking menace.
The world becomes alive in a nightmarish clarity of moving light,
as the white star slowly falls.

Now,
my feet frozen
and the dark shapes shifting around,
my rifle, my savior and love, dry and cold, slung behind,
arms burdened with linen for the cold Anbar night,
I want to look. My insides mutate. I stay frozen.
The fizzling sun continues to drop, the parachute swaying,
and dark things really dance now,
as I crane my neck to observe his bloated shell.

He waves to me, as if to say, "See you soon!" and my intestines climb my throat.
Fear surges, and my eyes sting with horror.
His arm in a blink becomes a cat, tail smoothly weaving the air,
its fangs mauling and devouring years of knowledge, which still lay nearby.
The feline ceases gorging, and begins cleaning itself,

starting with the paws, as the light extinguishes,
and I am once more alone with my friend in the darkness.

The darkness bound us.
I made other acquaintances in Fallujah,
but he stuck with me a long time,
waving from the concrete abyss,
black sockets under a crushed forehead,
living in the murky, forbidden chasms my rifle lusted after,
and in the deep cracks of my thoughts,
where memory is torture,
and the eyes of the dead roam free.

ALMOST TOO YOUNG SOLDIER WALKS THROUGH LOCAL TOWNSPEOPLE / ASH KYRIE

CORREGIDOR IN WAIT / RACHEL McNEILL

FIRE-ORE-BREATHER

IAN LAVALLEE

Singe me with shitting pellets down under my blouse.
My ears are drumming
Screaming.
Eyes bouncing, realigning.
Working with shoulder, arms and hands
to continue my belching flatulence.

Fire-ore-breather
Answer my flippant thumb and
First finger soft flesh squeezes
squeezes with follow through.
Release, Click,
Determined.
One sound, one motion
Blurred into one unit.

Fire-ore-breather
You I worship.
as a way through to some other plane.
I'm still here though
Never knowing your true
potential for me.

I AM THE SAVAGE

EMILY YATES

rubble beside the Tigris river
piled high above our waists
teeming with flies and also
the crumbling history of the world
tells me that this place is full of savages
but I am the savage

my eyes are dry until salty sweat
drips down the bridge of my nose
puddles in the corner of my lid
slides down my cheek
in place of tears
that don't well up in my eyes

we walk into proud homes
searching for those who would kill us
overturning bookshelves
as the wives and children of the accused
stand in the doorway with fearful faces
but I am not afraid

I wield the weapon of ignorance
I hide behind the shield of arrogance
I speak with the voice of entitlement

My job is to tell the story of victory —
victory!
Victory?
But I am defeated

ROAD TO RAMADI / EMILY YATES

IRAQI BOY v. HMMVW / EMILY YATES

IRAQI BIKE v. HMMVW / EMILY YATES

BAGHDAD JOINT PATROL / EMILY YATES

SICK EMPIRE

VICTOR INZUNZA

The sun in Al-Kut
scorches my star-spangled skin,
the palm groves are still,
and the silence is oppressive.

Yesterday, I saw children playing,
barefoot and smiling,
running beside the convoy. My mind
wanders there in its boredom.
I fight the fatigue

as I sit behind a loaded machine gun,
in a hole somewhere unimpressive.

My fingers are callous, palms
stained with filth.

My love waits back home,
as I wait like a starved dog

who will tear at your throat.
Waiting, unconcerned with
the distant decries of The Hill.

Their Fourth of July pageantry
will go on without us,
as we swing our fists in the air
at an empire swallowed by the sand,

swallowed by the fire,
and this mirage is all we know.

The sun falls above the rooftops,
and I think of women I saw
hanging laundry on the wire
above their homes.

Memories blast my mind, as
we paint the sand red, white, and blue,
for the sick empire.

MY TRIGGER FINGER

JUSTIN CLIBURN

I have never owned a gun larger than the Daisy BB gun that briefly held my interest when I was a child. The first time I fired a rifle was in basic training. To this day, after a one year tour of Baghdad, training exercises remain the only times I have fired a firearm. I still do not know if that is a result of my humanitarian spirit trumping my primal urge to fight or my trigger finger betraying me and my fellow soldiers.

One hot day in Baghdad, I was presented with two opportunities to put all that training into action and take a human life. I still have nightmares about what happened or, more accurately, what could have happened.

We were convoying down the familiar stretch of Route Irish that connected us to all we did in Baghdad, good and bad. It has been a relatively calm tour for the soldiers of the T-Bird 85 element and the calm was so unbelievable that we were starting to become stir-crazy. I, like always, was a gunner, and my primary job was to keep civilian traffic out of our convoy. As my truck reached the crest of the slowly rising hill and the on-ramp that funneled civilian traffic onto Route Irish, I peeked out over the turret. This was a relatively blind on-ramp for travelers merging onto Irish and I had to be extra vigilant.

Up from the ramp, at a speed that made all of us nervous, came a van that appeared to pay no attention to the U.S. Army convoy it was already dangerously close to. My heartbeat raced as I jumped and drew my weapon down on this possible VBIED[1]. From every truck, radio transmissions warned me of the advance and everyone's mind raced.

Was this the one?

Was this our time to feel the power of hundreds of pounds of explosives?

Was this our chance to strike first and take the fight to the enemy?

As I leaned further and further outside the turret, fists clenching my rifle as hard as I possibly could, I finally caught a glimpse of what was inside the ominous van. While paranoid soldiers yelled through the radio to fire, I made out a familiar scene. As perhaps seven or eight children horse-played in the rear of the van, a man navigated the vehicle while he rotated almost 180 degrees, screaming at them to knock it off. A woman sat to his right in the passenger seat and did the same.

I saw a man, a husband, a father, doing what he could to parent his children while a woman, a wife, a mother, did the same. As I realized what was happening, the shouts of fellow soldiers over the radio became more and more harassing. I did not want to shoot this man, this husband, this father, but by all measures of the rules of engagement, I had every right to.

As the anxiety of the situation reached its peak, the man finally turned around and saw me and the barrel of my M-4 carbine rifle staring him in the face. With rashness bordering on recklessness, the man sharply swerved to the shoulder as I made one last show of force and sat down, relieved.

I explained over the radio that the situation had been resolved and we continued our trek towards Traffic HQ[2]. At the entrance to the police station, traffic was blocked to allow us inside the compound. While my truck waited its turn to enter, a familiar IP[3] truck made its way toward the entrance from the opposite direction...towards the entrance and towards us. From where I stood, I could see the IP look me in the eye, point to the entrance, wave, and continue his advance. I yelled, I stood up, I pointed my weapon, but he kept on. With possibly the most aggressive posture I have ever used, I made one last attempt to show how serious I was, and it worked. The truck came to a screeching halt just a few feet from the entrance...and our lead truck.

Afterwards, our squad leader and our interpreter explained to the man in convincing fashion that he was lucky I had not killed him.

Later, one of my comrades approached me and asked why the fuck I hadn't shot that guy. I asked him which one. "Both of them!" he replied.

I told him about the van and the kids and father and family. I told him about the IP mistakenly believing he was an ally and could pass through, but my friend was undeterred and said both should have been shot to send a message.

Years after returning home, I still think about that day and, although the accompanying nightmares associated with that day have not reared their ugly head in months, the power that I had in my hands that day and many others still scares me.

I have dreamed of the exact same scenarios with variations. I have dreamed that I again do not pull the trigger and all my friends are killed thanks to a VBIED that I let through.

I have dreamed that my friend is the gunner and he shoots and kills a father and husband over one man's negligent driving.

I have dreamed that I pull the trigger, get congratulated by my teammates and am haunted for the rest of my life.

To this day, I do not know if I made a conscious decision based on principle or if I merely froze up and could not bring myself to fire on a human being. Both scenarios only lasted a matter of seconds but they'll stay with me for decades. It is because of my own experience in that situation that I will never think of another soldier's reaction to that scenario in terms of black and white. Life is not black and white and millions of shades of gray exist in the few seconds that make up the decision whether or not to fire when one is in a war zone.

---

[1] Vehicle-Born Improvised Explosive Device
[2] Headquarters
[3] Iraqi Police

TODAY I WATCHED TWO CHILDREN PLAY

JIM DALEY

One taunts and the other plays David
Or Daud

The tall, thin, brazen child of 15 years
Displays his wit and bravery
Calls out to the soldiers 20 yards distant
Mocks them and issues insults in his native tongue
He takes off his shoe and waves it at the soldiers
The crowd laughs, the soldiers become very angry
(The gravity of the insult eludes me)

He does not elude the sniper
One shot
The tall, thin, child of 15 years spends his last breath
In jest
Gripping in his hand, an instrument of offense

The short, thin, quiet child of 12 years
Displays his skill and courage
Places a stone in his sling and twirls it
Defies them and takes aim at the giants
He releases a stone that falls short of their vehicle
A soldier picks up the radio again, and I cry out
(The futility of the act eludes me)

He does not elude the sniper
One shot
The short, thin, quiet child of 12 years spends his last breath
In Anger
Lying near his twisted form is an instrument, of defense?

Offense, defense, security — right? wrong.
Two kids...

THEY CALLED ME BOBBY / TOBY HARTBARGER

BAGHDAD'S MOST CONVENIENT BANK / TOBY HARTBARGER

THE IRAQIS WEAR THE WAR IN BAGS UNDER THEIR EYES

PATRICK MAJID DOHERTY

That afternoon
I escorted the mourning parents
Using my weapon to point them along the boot-beaten path
To the Aid Station.
The child lay in a supine position
Littered on a litter.
The men wore Arabic Dishdashas[1],
Kanzus[2] in Swahili,
Man-dresses in American.
The women were clad in black,
The liturgical garb women wore
when I was a child in Kenya.
A common uniform,
Its dye made the women who wore it
Always ready for a funeral.
The women sobbed in Iraqi.
Me and the Sudanese,
The other translator,
Our families beyond the border,
Traded hits on a hash pipe that night
And shared dreams,
Our flags at half staff,
Their poles formed straight lines,
One longer than the other,
Easterly and westerly from the Sudanese at forty
And the American, still a teen,
Between the bodies
Of the men from three sides
Who had fallen
In the Sunni Triangle of Death[3].

---

[1] ankle-length garment, usually with long sleeves, similar to a robe, commonly worn in Arab countries.
[2] long, usually white garment worn by men in Africa
[3] the area between Baghdad and Al Hillah inhabited by a Sunni majority that contains several large towns in the Mahmudiya District, including Yusufiyah, Mahmoudiyah, Iskandariyah and Latifiyah

HAPPY BIRTHDAY

ZACHARIAH DEAN

I get together every now and again with a close friend whose been
around the bend.
He's put his time in and he's managed to see it through to the end.
We usually drink, laugh, chit chat about bullshit we've been in at
different points in the past.
I asked if he could lend some helpful advice on the subject of a
certain foreign land
in which I will soon have many months to spend.
He emptied his face and cleared his throat and till this day I can
still hear the quote and it echoes.
His words were precise and stung like ice as he spoke.
He simply stated with faded eyes and with a nervousness in his breath:
Afghanistan was "no joke" and on that note I chose to change the subject.

Flash forward half a year.
Wrap me in Kevlar[1] and sapi[2].
Change the face in the mirror.
Bathe me in sweat and sprinkle me with discontent and subtle fear.
When I flip the latch and kick the hatch open to expose the vast dirt terrain
this desolate place holds in its mold only certain hurt and pain.
This harsh and unforgiving landscape thrives off swallowing a man's weight.
The heat makes the pounds difficult to keep and that's just the meat
the insects don't eat.
I've gotten weak and somewhere a year ago fell deep asleep.
Now I've woke to a place where you have to investigate every single
step you take.
So for the sake of safety I find it's best to just stay awake because
sleep is too difficult of a feat to seize under circumstances such as
these.

As a Combat Engineer
My role was made perfectly clear.
Friendly death tolls can ride solely on these shoulders out here.
I shudder to think that it's solely up to me
to know and avoid all accidents that could come to be.
Some baby back home could have a father that's forever absent
Because I got lazy and I can't have that happen.
I hate to have to explain to some mourning mother that her son was slain
simply because in that moment I wasn't on my game.
So I stay suspicious of every discolored piece of dust or rock that
seems to be missing.

I keep a pace count because the grounds been known to leap up and eat men from the waist down.

Today I have to skip all that.
I must make haste.
Marines are on the bank waiting.
I'm late for a firefight to chase.
Leap from the charm that is mounted armor.
Removal of safety makes me all the more shaky in the face of harm.
I'm calling in my due for good karma.
Boots are engulfed and hidden by a cloud of loose dust that's emitted.
It's the terrain's way of saying it can't be trusted and I find that fitting.
I've begun my run across what one would be too bold to call Earth.
The Sun is furnace that never stops burning through my shirt.
My gear and steps are as heavy as my breaths.
To this day I don't know what separates life and death.
Or the line between being superstitious and religious
I just cross my chest when I make my wishes.
And this foolish sprint is one of those instances.
Praise God by day and cover up the light on my iPod at night.
I doubt it's a phase; either way, makes me feel better, makes me right.
I'm moving up on the Marines and slam my back against the embankment.
The young Marine next to me smiles and says he's glad I could make it.
I fake the motivation.
In these moments I don't know what to state smartly.
So I just quote an 80's action movie and say
"You think I'd miss this party?"

The Sergeant screams; "Stand by to fire upon the tree line."
"Marines one and three on my command; stand, I'm sure that fuckin' ditch is manned."
"Marines two and four; observe and await further orders we have to get these fuckin' hadji's shooting mortars."
"Marines one and three...do your thing."
I stand and with my non-firing hand wipe the sweat from eyes so I can see.
And I don't see any enemies but medium machine gun fire starts to find me.
I pull the trigger and it clicks.
Fuck! Son of a bitch! Motherfucker, now I got to take cover and fix this shit.
I dip down and slam back against the berm.
Curse as I attempt to learn the cause to this problem.
It's turned my day from bad to worse.
My metallic boomstick flower needs its brass seeds of malice;
otherwise I'm powerless.
It seems the rounds didn't feed.
It could be anything.
I'm fishing through the possibilities;
Lack of lub, bolt's full of sand, bad mag spring, something missing.
The list endless in these harsh conditions.

I remove the mag fast when my left hand crosses my eye's path.
My wrist watch is telling me that more than time must be lost.
Perhaps my mind is crossed.
The timepiece holds what I should have always known.
Under the seconds that flip
It's June 18th and I'm here in the worst way when it finally hits.
Happy Birthday, Dean; You're 26.

I should be somewhere double-fisting glasses of whiskey getting tipsy.
Instead I'm wishing the enemy keeps missing.
Fuck. You know what?
It's all good.
My situation hasn't changed much.
I enlisted, I never thought I would make it to 26 anyway.
It was either this or continually clench my fist to avoid assisting
these wrists with slits.
Now I'm just sitting in the shit attempting to fix my ballistics.
So fuck it.
It's a nice thought though, being back home.
But back to the task at hand.
Got to find the issue that caused my jam and stick to the plan.

Focus
What a mess but problem found.
Just my luck; a dented round
stuck under the chamber.
Exchange for a fresh mag and slam it down.
Feel like I'm out of danger.
Rack the bolt back and listen for that soothing sound.
A perfectly functioning weapon is a force to be reckoned.
Now; close eyes, deep breath, calm hands that quiver, clear all the
thoughts of home that I'm missing,
restate prayers and wishes, turn, stand and deliver.

I wrote this in a hurry in a machine gun turret several nights later.
Try to burn it out of memory by putting it on paper.
I'm not sure anybody else heard it.
But now I have that same nervousness in my breath
I first heard in my friend that last time we met.
And the joke's on me.
Because I can only see the Marines that are suffering.
The Shepherd passes by and whistles as we pepper his land with missiles.
It's an amusing business this death dealing.
Because winning a war has never felt more like losing feeling.

---

1 protective material found in military jackets or helmets
2 Small Arms Protective Inserts

BOOTS IN THE MUD

AARON NEWSOM

Boots in the mud
With traces of blood
Dripping urine
Cause the shit is what we're in
Trying to hold back the urge for mourning
At least till morning
Stirs in the distance
Wishes of relevance
And thoughts of relatives
While in the presence of hostages
Trying to change minds
While kicking dirt over mines
And in the sand drawing lines
Claiming we have the rights to the finds
Searching for the fountain of youth
While speaking like we're the fountain of truth
Lost is the past
And the stories of our grandfathers
Now we're just lost little sons and daughters

MUSINGS FROM A 25 YEAR OLD MILITARY POLICE SERGEANT IN IRAQ

Or, How the hell did I end up here and when can I go home already?

KELLY DOUGHERTY

10 July 2003, month 4 of the U.S. occupation

I do realize that, when I do write in my journal, I usually don't write about the present, about what is actually happening in real life, here in Iraq. I guess that is because I hate being here so much and feel conflicted, hypocritical, and weak. So, instead I regress into daydreams. Well, the moon has finally made a comeback this past week. It started out as a fingernail clipping offset to the left by the pinprick of light that is the Evening Star. Then it looked like the eye of that sad owl we found. Now it is bright white, half of the face showing. I really like how the "man in the moon" really looks like a face.

The trees here are amazing. How they can be alive is a testament to the will to survive. They are tall and bent from the wicked winds, limbs and long needles hanging limply from their leeward sides. "Green" would not be an accurate color to describe them. Rather, they are grey, brown, tannish, and olive drab. They look as though a giant grabbed them by their trunks, tore them out by their roots, and violently beat the ground with them repeatedly. In a rage, knocking off needles and branches, and bending the limbs and covering the trees with dust. Then the angry giant calmed and jammed the trees back into the ground.

Everything here looks half dead, hot and starved, and waiting for an opportunity to die or escape. The skinny, panting fox with the ridiculously big ears who stole bread from our truck, the big owl with the orange saucer eyes that gave up and died of heartache and old age, and the camels that plod slowly and awkwardly through the desert, knock-kneed with dreadlocks of fur, their faces perpetually looking dopey, but with a smile. The Iraqi people have the same desperate look because of a life of hardships from every direction. Poverty, hunger, war, and heat. Everything makes them have sketchiness about them. It is as if they are equally likely to cut your throat for the bottle of water in your hand as they are to warn you of a planned attack against you and your troops, and then invite you into their house for tea and a nice meal. And this could be the same person.

The kids are all skin and bones. They do not wear shoes or go to school. They know just enough English to beg for water and food and look young for their ages with too-big heads and eyes that look too old for children. Boys you could swear are only nine or ten have mustaches. There was one guy selling ice and stuff at the fuel point. He had the most amazing eyes. They were pale blue, milky, and obscure, like thoughts of a hidden lagoon. I don't know, that sounds dumb, but I've never seen eyes like that before.

I am really only ever sort of happy when I am not working. And, oh goddamn, I have to go back to work tomorrow. Shit! It's patrols. I hate g.d. patrols. They are risky business. I do not like dealing with the Iraqis. I loathe it, disdain, abhor, hate, etc., etc. Maybe I will have sweet dreams tonight and they will leave me feeling happy when I wake up.

ALL CLEAR

DAVID MANN

The Alarm sounds
Lightning, Lightning, Lightning

All I want to do is eat my meal in peace
But with the fear of WMD's, I don my protective gear
"8 minutes or else" the army says
No one takes 8 minutes

Thousands of men and women, silent
A giant mess hall
Frozen
No one joked, no one said a word
It would be a lie to say these men and women were without fear
They were terrified

Meanwhile, sweat pools around my face
Goddamn gas mask is so hot, so god awful sweaty
In this gear,
Everyone looks the same
Faceless and emotionless
Thousands of scared, lifeless soldiers

Are they thinking of home?
Or the meal that was interputed?
Are they thinking about WMD's?
Or how fuckin' hot this NBC[1] gear is?

Finally
All clear, All clear, All clear
Now the place erupts
Masks are removed
Chairs squeak as they are pushed in
Madness, as everyone rushes for the door

Eventually, people will joke about this becoming routine, alarms with no attacks.
Routine or not, I taste the fear

---

[1] Nuclear, Biological, and Chemical

DUST MEMORIES
AARON HUGHES

LANDSCAPE

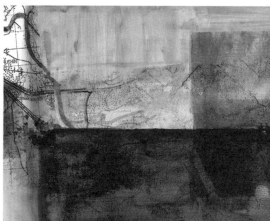

EUPHRATES RIVER CROSSING

DEPLOY

ON THE BANKS OF THE EUPHRATES

JOSIAH WHITE

Our patrol was supposed to be a normal one: circle around north of the city and return back, looking out for any suspicious individuals. In June, the heat of Iraq is oppressive. Our bulky flak jackets and helmets did not help much.

I was stationed in the rear of the patrol after screwing up too many times at the front on other patrols. My job was to periodically turn around and make sure nothing weird was happening behind us. I had already perfected the art of walking backwards without stumbling, no easy task when laden with sixty plus extra pounds.

Nothing particularly interesting happened until we reached the apex of our circular loop. A few stray dogs were wandering around causing trouble, threatening to bite someone if we didn't keep our eyes on them. One dog was especially daring and slowly inched his way towards me every time I turned to face the rest of the patrol. I grew tired of the dog and tried to shoo it away by throwing rocks at him, but he never left.

The sergeant leading the patrol came back and asked why I was holding up the patrol. The sergeant and I assaulted the dog with any rock we could find. He eventually took the hint and hobbled off, finally leaving me in peace. We continued on until someone near the front halted us again. I took my regular position: crouched on one knee angled slightly to the rear, so that I could observe what was happening up front and behind. I stayed in that position for a long time. The Marines in the front of the patrol were doing something, but I didn't know what. Then it trickled back: the point-man had found an IED.

Improvised Explosive Device, a pedantic name for the most lethal thing a lone patrol could encounter on the streets of Iraq. This wasn't the first time I had been on a patrol when we discovered something like this. Up to this point, they had all turned out to be a box of wires or some other misplaced tool. The suspected IED looked like someone took a mortar round and cut off the top half of the dome, leaving the guiding fins in place, then welded a piece of metal where the half-dome had been. If anyone wanted to design a decent IED, this was it.

There were no wires leading to it or antennas sticking out. We felt fairly confident that it would not go off unexpectedly. The question was: what to do with it? We certainly couldn't put it back where we found it, and we didn't want to take it back to base. We called the explosive experts and they told us they were too busy to deal with such a small thing. Our navigator suggested we hike out to the Euphrates River and throw it in. The sergeant agreed.

I didn't have a map and didn't know how far it was to the river. I assumed it was only a few minutes away. We turned down a dirt road leading between a fenced grove of trees and a lush green open field, a very rare sight in Iraq. I checked my water and saw I was running a little low. The sweat on my forehead continued to rain down unabated.

The natural pace of a patrol is very slow. Our job was to show the residents of the city that we were here and had guns, but not present ourselves as easy targets for snipers or anyone else. This natural slow pace is aggravating to someone with low water and no idea why a lengthy detour is taken.

No one tells the guy in the back what is happening. All I knew was that when I turned around, no one was there holding a gun to my face, and that is how I liked it. We came up on the river, surprising some local fishermen in their boats. The sergeant took the IED and threw it directly in to the current, sinking it forever. Some of the Iraq army soldiers we were training in our patrol wanted to take a break and buy some fish. I wanted to take off all of my clothes and jump into the river. No one got what they wanted.

As we laboriously hiked back to our regular route I wondered about what we had thrown into the river. Suppose it was an explosive device. The water would slowly erode the casing, exposing the chemicals inside. With time they would dissolve into the water and float downstream. I had patrolled by the Euphrates many times and was constantly struck by the magnificent beauty of the natural oasis on its shores. Farmers grew crops using sophisticated irrigation techniques and modern equipment. Ranchers relied on the water to raise their cows and goats. For thousands of years, perhaps longer, this ancient river sustained generations of people. Now here we were throwing explosives into it.

This was in 2006, three years into the war and infinity before it ended. How many explosives were thrown into the river, either by troops on the ground, the bombers in the air, or the newly established insurgency? The effect of all this pollution wouldn't be noticed right away; maybe no one would connect the dots. That explosive material will find its way to the shore and into the crops. A thirsty donkey will gulp it down regardless of the strange metallic taste. Decades down the road, a young man like me will jump in the cool river to escape the heat and a little bit of it will be absorbed into his skin. The casualties of this war are destined to increase through the ages.

We finally made it back to our regular route. By this time I was completely out of water and felt a little dizzy. The symptoms of heat exhaustion had been drilled into my brain. Heavy sweating — this was less of a symptom than a daily fact of life — tiredness, cramps, a tingling feeling in the extremities. Was I feeling these or just imagining them? I looked at my fellow Marines to see if they felt the same way. Everyone had the same sweat-soaked grim face.

We patrolled a little more until other Marines spoke up; they were out of water, too. On average we carried nearly a gallon of water per person. I drank every last drop within an hour and still felt thirsty. One of the Iraqi soldiers suggested we knock on doors of the houses near us and demand they give us water. We didn't have many options. We were still an hour out of base and no one was coming to pick us up. The first house we visited had a family inside. The Iraqi soldier spoke in a very quick and demanding Arabic and soon someone came with a cool two liter bottle of water. We gathered the family together near the entrance of the house so none of them could try anything funny. The sergeant singled me out as the most exhausted of us all and told me to go inside and drink. Once in the house I reflexively sat down and took off my helmet to let my head cool. The family stared at me with wide eyes.

The sergeant yelled at me to get up and put my helmet back on. We weren't supposed to show weakness in front of the townsfolk. Trying to stay cool is a weakness. Outside, the bottle of water was passed around and was soon gone. We gave the empty bottle back and patrolled on. With one less bottle of water, would the family be forced to drink from the Euphrates, or was what we just drank from there in the first place? The water helped a bit, enough that everyone was able to make it back to base without collapsing on the roadside.

After the debriefing I took off all of my gear and sat down with just shorts on. My buddy handed me a sealed bottle of water from a crate. We had a whole crate filled to the brim with bottles of water shipped from who-knows-where. Despite being in the shade the water was still around 90 degrees, but the temperature did little to dissuade me; I drank it quickly and mechanically. I didn't think of how clean it was. I didn't think of the pile of good food we had. I didn't think back to my home and how it wasn't in the middle of a war zone. I didn't think about how safe I was going to be once I made it back, about the long life I am going to live. Instead I drank as the sweat flowed down my chest like a mighty ancient river, collecting all of the dust and salt and whisking it away forever.

SPENT / MICHAEL DAY

LOST / RACHEL McNEILL

SHEPHERDS / RACHEL McNEILL

THE IRAQI WARD

FREDERICK FOOTE

for Mounira

A village always suffers
this one had gowns
old men tea drinkers
there were prayers
and dominoes
and cards though only
half the players had hands

All those were games
you watched but wouldn't play
you were the muse there
smiling mound
in a black burqah
you left your face unveiled
who would hide
such beaming eyes
such rounded cheeks away

Your children dead
within the riddled car
and yet you never cried
when we made scarves
you tied one on
the girl who couldn't move
you led the prayers
certified the food
and never once broke down

Until the day
the place was disassembled
the healed taken
out to crouching Frogs
for transport home
that was the day you chose
to fall into the arms
of Senior-Chief Minata
the one so good with the kids
a man not your husband
to sway weeping
clasped together
a strange beast
half uniformed half black
crying "Salaam, Salaam!"

CONVERSATION / ASH KYRIE

SKULL MASK C130 / ASH KYRIE

NO YOU CAN'T SHOOT THEM

MARIO FIGUEROA

I am a Marine. I have been deployed to Iraq to, as my Commander-In-Chief told the world: "Fight them over there, so we don't have to fight them here." I still was not sure why we had to fight the Iraqis at all. But then I have never been one much for fighting. However, what scared me more then fighting a war was the Abyss that I imagined swallowing my humanity if I were to take another man's life. Is that not what happened to the Vietnam vets? Did the Abyss not swallow them after the horrible things their country asked them to do? I was not opposed to doing my duty, nor protecting my fellow Marine brothers, I just did not want to lose my humanity in the process. While in the desert, I walked with constant fear and vigilance, lest I fall into that Abyss.

My unit had been in country for several months, conducting all sorts of raids, patrols, and humanitarian efforts (reestablishing water lines, providing security for various infrastructure projects). On several of these missions I had returned fire, but to my knowledge I had never killed a man. I was okay with that. This particular night my squad was deployed to a designated OP[1], which overlooked a main supply route that had been previously targeted with roadside bombs.

Any Marine can tell you that it is not Al-Qaeda, not the Taliban, that are his worst enemy. It is the roadside bomb. Relentless in its mission, ruthless in its execution; the roadside bomb cannot surrender nor can it listen to reason. It exists only to kill. It does not care if it is captured or destroyed; the operational force of the United States Military in all its destructive glory does not sway it. If it could it would laugh at all our might, because with all our power we are unable to deter the roadside bomb from executing its mission. However, the roadside bomb cannot act alone, it needs an accomplice to assemble its components and to place it where it may do its deadly deed. Tonight we are tasked with killing the men who helped this abomination into existence and aided it in its terrible execution.

We arrived at our destination and dismounted the HMMWV[2] — or as she is commonly referred to — Humvee. This was not a firefight; this was deliberately putting a bullet into the brain of an unsuspecting man. This was the Abyss. I imagined this must be what snipers feel like. Being a sniper lost some of its romanticism that night. Despite my moral and ideologically born trepidation over my mission at that time, our Intel stated that these men were in league with the enemy and had been killing Marines. No matter my hesitation I firmly believed that to kill a Marine was to sign your death warrant. This inner justification helped edge myself closer to the endless darkness of the Abyss.

I was to choose one of the Marines from my team and take him to the top of the OP and wait for the men who would place the great enemy of the Marines.

We would kill the men and destroy the enemy; truly a noble mission done in the names of every Marine that had fallen unsuspecting to an enemy who refused to fight him face to face. I told myself this over and over again. However, I was constantly in fear that my humanity would be consumed, and that I would be turned into a broken shell of a man similar to those dejected soldiers that had returned from Vietnam.

So I chose Lance Corporal Smith. I chose him because he was reliable. I chose him because he carried an automatic light machine gun that could place a wall of lead in between trouble and us, should trouble find us. But the main reason I chose Lance Corporal Smith was because he wanted it. He wanted to jump head first into the Abyss and he did not even know it was there. And I hated him for it. I told myself that if he actually had to kill someone he would shut his fucking mouth about it and his arrogance to the subject would haunt him for all his days. If all went as planned Smith would be sacrificed to the Abyss, and I would stay on the edge for one more day.

So we trekked up the rock formation in silence, as we were maintaining tactical discipline, but I could see the anticipation in his eyes, the bloodlust.

Smith and I scanned the target area with our NVG[3]'s as we heard the rumbling of a motorcycle engine approaching. My heartbeat quickened, the sweat from my brow trickled down my face and my finger instinctively curled around the trigger of my M16A2 service rifle. Through my NVG's I saw two Iraqi men of fighting age (whatever that means anymore) on the motorcycle as they enter the target area. I looked over at Smith.

He is excited, anxious, nervous, but most of all he wants to kill. Smith is not a bad person; he wants to do his job so badly that he does not see the darkness swirling around us. He does not hear the voices from the Abyss cackling as they goad me into giving the order that pushes Smith over the edge.

I wanted to give the order; I wanted to sacrifice Smith and save myself. It took everything I had to whisper to Smith to hold his fire until we see what these two men are going to do. He gave me a look that plainly stated, "What the fuck do you think they are going to do?" But still I waited, as something did not feel right.

The motorcycle came to a stop and the two men, looking as nervous and anxious as Smith, were moving in a suspiciously covert way. They had to be on a mission to kill Marines. I switched the safety of my rifle to the fire position and give Smith the thumbs-up. Thumbs-up meant prepare to fire, thumbs-down and these men would meet their end and the Abyss would claim another victim.

As I prepared to give Smith the thumbs-down something happened that I would never forget. One of the men turned his back to the other, paused, looked to his left and then to his right, undid his trousers and bent over. The second man undid his trousers as well and stepped up to the bent over man and began to fuck the shit out of him! He just went to town on this guy and both Smith and I looked up from our sights, popped up our NVG's, and looked at each other with a mix of astonishment, disbelief and incredulousness. It took everything we had not to break sound discipline and start rolling on the ground laughing our tails off.

Then perhaps the most ridiculous moment in my combat experience happened—Smith looked at me with wide-eyed innocence mixed with utter confusion and asks with a stutter, "Do...do I shoot them?" I know the Abyss is listening for my response. "NO you can't shoot them dumb shit, do you want to to prison!" My world was spinning around me. I was here to send Smith into the Abyss as he painted the desert sand with bad guy brains and here instead were two Iraqi men going all "Don't Ask, Don't Tell" on each other in my goddamn target zone!

I went to the top of that OP believing that my humanity was at stake and was willing to sacrifice Smith to protect it. It was easy to justify because Smith was so young and ignorant to the perils of taking a human life. I should have warned him about the dangerous path he was on, but he would not have listened anyway, and we all must learn these terrible truths for ourselves.

I would eventually kill another man. It was everything I feared it to be, but to my surprise I found that the Abyss had not consumed me. I still maintained my idealism and my empathy for human life, but I was one of the lucky ones. I was lucky not only for having crawled out of the Abyss with my humanity but for being able to witness the midnight rendezvous of these two forbidden lovers whose actions helped remind me, when I needed it most, why that humanity was worth retaining.

---

[1] Observation Point
[2] High Mobility Multipurpose Wheeled Vehicle
[3] Night Vision Goggles

THE SURREALIST MOVEMENT IN THE MIDDLE EAST

PAUL WASSERMAN

Soldier in a sports coat, Kuwait International Airport
Just another chauffeur at the arrivals gate
Holding up his AMERICAN THEATER sign
Marshalling us back to the zone after R&R[1]

Shipment of dogs to the Combat Stress Center
At last the Army practicing shaman medicine
In the event of an approaching breakdown
Personnel may drop by the CSC and pet the dogs

Mandatory rules of engagement briefing
Hundreds in the pews of the base chapel
JAG[2] officer standing under a display of the Christ
Ends each mock scenario, "Is it alright to kill now?"

Rack of reissued pulp novels in the main PX[3]
Their cover paintings a vision of the perfect binge
Following a summer love suicide on Ninth Avenue
While transiting between targets in Mosul

Fellow sergeant, longtime San Francisco
Letter carrier shorts, Clash t-shirt, and pistol harness
Brewing a batch of beer on a charcoal grill
Leaning in, "So who plays me in the movie?"

---

[1] Rest and Relaxation
[2] Judge Advocate General
[3] Post Exchange

MISSION ACCOMPLISHED

JENNIFER PACANOWSKI

The banner waved proudly, "Mission Accomplished"

The statue came crashing down as the crowd cheered
Crumbling a dictatorship
As democracy ruptured onto the scene

I signed my name in the blood of dead children that I was yet to know of
My word, My promise.
My vow binding my life like an Asian woman's feet
A choice?
They yell, your choice
No draft forcing your unwilling trembling hand to sign
Was it a choice or an order?
Abusing the children of a forgotten country of survivors
The children begging for candy being ripped through convoy wheels
Stripping flesh from bone
MEDIC!!!
Nothing left but the RPG's[1] flying overhead like bottle rockets on the
fourth of July
Independence, Freedom, my choice, my choice to kill

They scream, "Traitor!"
YOU, "Iraq Veteran Against the War"
"How can you be against your fellow soldiers and marines?"
Tears design my camouflage.
I am against the war and for Life.
For, FORE, FOUR!!!
My words sting like a golf ball whizzing into your face

Anger and hatred is now my contagious disease
Don't look in my eyes
The cynicism and the lack of belief in my government
Will burn you and cause you to see the truth
Interrupting your happy care bear world with all your smart opinions on
the war
The war, YOU never fought

WAR

Before the war my eyes shone with hope and optimism

An idealism that I could make a difference
and maybe, just maybe, save people

Instead I stand here on my homeland soil
Listening to your fancy ideas and lies about the war
THE WAR THAT I FOUGHT!

And every time they vote for the continuation of this needless and
unfounded war
They vomit the blood of my fellow fallen soldiers and marines

---

[1] Rocket Propelled Grenade

ONE EACH
GRAHAM CLUMPNER

ACU Cap Patrol	One Each
Coat Army Combat Uniform (ACU)	One Each
Trousers Army Combat Uniform (ACU)	One Each
Boot Hot Weather Tan (Pair)	One Each
Belt, Riggers Black	One Each
Bag, Waterproof	One Each
Knee Pads, Desert (Two)	One Each
Glove System (Nomex)	One Each
Advanced Combat Helmet (Tan)	One Each
Canteen (2 Quart)	One Each
Pack, Field Large	One Each
Entrenching tool	One Each
Neck Gaiter	One Each
Ballistics Glasses	One Each
Mask Protective (Gas)	One Each
Chemical Decontamination Kit	One Each
M4A1 Rifle	One Each
Deployment (OEF[1], OIF[2])	One Each
Traumatic Brain Injury (TBI)	One Each
Nightmares	One Each
Post Traumatic Stress Disorder (PTSD)	One Each
Bible (Army Issue, Camouflage)	One Each
Military Sexual Trauma (MST)	One Each
Anxiety	One Each
Spousal Abuse	One Each
Rejection	One Each
Hate	One Each
Depression	One Each
Loneliness	One Each
Suicide	One Each

[1] Operation Enduring Freedom
[2] Operation Iraqi Freedom

THE THINGS WE CARRIED

DAVID MANN

I carried a saw
I was not a carpenter

I carried two rifles
even though I did not want one

I carried a machine gun
yet I was not a killer

I carried fear
I was afraid

I carried dirt
I was not a farmer

I carried a radio
I was not a DJ

I carried the fiery Mesopotamian sun
I did not tan

I carried body armor
it did not protect

I carried sandbags
it did not stop the flood

I carry pain
I am a veteran

"Most clearly of that battle I remember
The tiredness in eyes, how hands looked thin
Around a cigarette, and the bright ember
Would pulse with all the life there was within."

Louis Simpson, World War II Veteran
—from "The Battle"

THE BLOW OF MEMORY'S RETURN

"I visited your country one day,
Bomb blasts and bullet shells...
I'm only here to help.
. . .
I'm having a hard time sleeping tonight,
Chronic pain and bad dreams...
I want you to forgive me."

Eli Wright, Iraq Veteran, Warrior Writer
—from "Shock and Awe"

THESE BOOTS

AMBER STONE

These boots were never comfortable
and they always meant work.
I must have been crazy to want a pair
so desperately.
Little did I know they
would change my life forever.
I loved my boots though.
Took great pride in the fabulous shine.
Tramped all over South Korea.
That sure was a good time,
yet lots of training—I was glad to leave
behind.
They've been everywhere man.
Georgia was the next stop.
These boots.
These boots are tan;
stained with the sandy dirt, sewage, and blood.
Not my blood.
That sentence makes me smile.
Not a smile energized with happiness,
rather gratefulness—for it wasn't me.
These boots have walked upon the Holy Land.
But I couldn't find anything holy about it.
These boots have become a part of me.
I have grown comfortable in these boots,
and they comfort me.
These boots carry me from place to place.
These boots have a story.
One they'll never tell.

BLACK OUT DRIVE

GARETT REPPENHAGEN

Follow the tail lights
The road fades into green pitch
Broken lines like memories,
your traumatic brain injury must stitch
Slipping in and out,
"Maaaannnnn, that's just the meds."
You wake up and you're home,
but you're homeless, half dead.
Up all night,
to howl at the moon.
Back in your rack,
Asleep till noon.
One thousand night missions,
since your separation.
Pre-combat checks,
with no expectations.
Put on your boots, your tags and your cover.
Another anti-parade march.
"Heeeey, welcome home brother."
Just grip that wheel hero.
Stay alert, stay alive.
The real war has just started,
Your fight to survive.

SPLICED

ZACH LAPORTE

My life is like a slide show, spliced with images of the desert.
Mom asks me if I like the potatoes,
      A woman shrieks from a bloodied mouth.
My Professor hands me an exam paper,
      I'm riding in the door of a Blackhawk.
I walk alone at night past neon signs,
      Crimson tracers snap so close you could touch.
I sit in my air-conditioned cubicle,
      The blood in my brain boils.
The scars run deeper than they appear.

A DISCONNECT AS WIDE AS THE OCEAN
GRAHAM CLUMPNER

[An excerpt from an account of a bad night at a bar shortly after coming home from a combat deployment in Afghanistan]...

Did you kill anyone? How was it over there? Was it hot? Are you fucking kidding me? I get more diverse questions at the DMV than when I came back from war. At first I thought I could explain it, thought that I could maybe bridge the gap between those who served and those who hadn't. But after about three sentences I began to notice that people lose interest. At that point I don't even want to talk anymore; if they can't pay attention to my answer for a minute after they ask the question then I'm not interested in telling them about it. I never told Jack what happened that night at the bar. I almost felt like it would be too much of a burden for him if I could ever find a way to truly explain it.

Most Americans just want to stay detached, to keep the deployed world separate from the home world. There is a general lack of sympathy for people who voluntarily wanted to go to war. The theory goes: why should we feel sorry for people who put themselves in that position, we didn't force them, they chose on their own. This feeling is felt by those in the military as they generally keep their experiences to themselves, feeling guilty for what they've seen and more for what they have done. These wars have lost their novelty, it is no longer a really fun video game to watch on the nightly news. Now it's just an annoying burden that keeps people from watching their favorite reality show.

When I was coming close to leaving the war all I could think about was getting home, drinking an ice cold beer, getting a blow job and never taking orders from anyone ever again. Now that I was in the environment where I could have all these things I didn't care. I had nothing in common with these people. Jack hadn't noticed it yet but I was not the same person I had been when I left. I couldn't live around people who walk on eggshells around me and I resolved as he dropped me off that night, that I would never speak of what I had seen to anyone ever again.

THE MONSTER I BECAME

ROBYNN MURRAY

It was a picturesque moment when I realized what a monster I had become. I was sitting in my mother's car in our small town waiting for her to come out of the pharmacy. The sun was shining and the grass was shimmering. I looked up and standing under the waving American flag was a woman and her granddaughter. It looked like a Norman Rockwell painting.

In Iraq I pointed my weapons at families all the time. It was made "ok" for me because they were different. They were made my enemy, they were brown, they were hajiis[1], they weren't American to me or even human, so it didn't matter.

Thinking of the faces of those people and how I stripped them of their humanity, tears started pouring down my cheeks and I felt like dying.

When my mother came out, I was in full hysterics slumped over in my seat. She asked me what was wrong and tried her best to comfort me. I couldn't tell her the truth, because I was afraid she would see the monster I had become and be unable to love me anymore.

---

[1] Arabic word (spelled haji, hajji, or hadji) for someone who has made the pilgrimage to Mecca; slang/derogatory term used by some U.S. military personnel for Iraqis, or anyone of Arab or Afghan descent

WHITEHAUS

IAN J. LAVALLEE

La ilaha il Allah, Muhammadur Rasullallah[1]
My Life for four months in the sandbox
Playing 300 meter drop dancer
Hoping to meet you by chance, at last?!
Together my brother or blood suicide sister.
I want your purple mist of desperation
puffed on my
only naked face
tasted and savored forever
to teach me to live like a man
to make me cry all of you out
on my sunken, below eye bluebags
into my lazy beard
to disappear
even for myself.
I never saw it, I never felt it,
Your Finger
drawing down my cheeks,
or bouncing off,
supersonic bruises left for pretend.

---

[1] Translation: "There is no god but God, and Muhammad is the messenger of God" (Arabic)

INJURED POCKETS

VARTAN GUBBINS

Good days pass without torment
of landing mortars.

I forget to pump gas into my fuel efficient car,
bills and credit card dues stacked high.
Nothing will happen if I just sit here
surfing the internet a little while longer.

Landing after landing near our building
awakens soldiers from afternoon naps.

A neighbor slams a door
below my second floor apartment
to muffle the sound inside.
They must be arguing again
about his late night binges.
Her yelling keeps me up at night —
                     I'm jealous of them.
Friends stopped asking me about dust
on my clothes,
and in my pad.

Night after night metal pulverizes stiff
desert near our T-walled living quarters,
concrete slabs that square
around our compound to protect us.

Vehicles of death fly, sit, walk
to cause our fall in final defeat,
an uneasy endeavor we endure day to day.
The envelopes stack sharply in my room.

My injured pockets are inhibited
to speak valued words —
my broke merit of eloquence.

COFFEE BREAK

BRENNAN BECK

I look around as I sit alone in the back of a crowded coffee shop, the corner of the walls pressed securely against my back. I sip on my blazing cup of coffee, burning the tip of my tongue with every taste.

Across the room sits a group of four young adults about my age. They're deep in conversation, talking about books they've read or people they knew. I watch jealously as they laugh at each other's striking words, losing themselves in the moment.

One of the girls glances up and meets my eyes. I look away shyly. After a few moments of staring at the dirt collected at the tip of my boot, I glance back up. The girl and her friends are now back in their conversation, this time talking about a recent movie that didn't disappoint or a new song they heard on the radio. They certainly weren't talking about how four years ago this day PFC[1] Chad Marsh was killed by the blast of a hand grenade in NE[2] Baghdad.

I sat there, staring enviously, imagining that in another life I could've been sitting there with them, laughing carelessly at unrehearsed conversations, enjoying the warmth of friends while sipping away at my cup of joe. I imagine that, in another life, we could go down the street to the theater and watch the new action movie, mimicking the hero's cheesy phrases and losing ourselves in laughter. I imagine we could share a joint in the park and reveal our greatest hopes and deepest secrets openly with each other and become philosophers in the process.

Maybe in another life where I hadn't lost my best friend at nineteen by the hands of a cowardly enemy, hearing his screams for help as the medic stuffed medical gauze into the softball-sized hole in his lower abdomen. Maybe in another life where I hadn't shot down an Iraqi man with an M240B machine gun as I pumped round after round after round into his dying body until finally he laid lifeless in the street. Maybe in another life where I hadn't lost fourteen Brothers in Arms and been filled with an endless rage that lays dormant but never really goes away.

Maybe in another life...

But not this one.

So I sit here alone and burn my tongue.

---

[1] Private First Class
[2] Northeast

OPEN WOUND

ELI WRIGHT

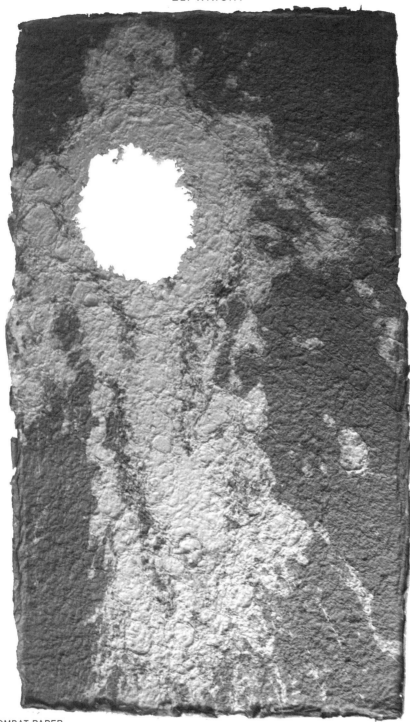

COMBAT PAPER

EVERY NIGHT

ZACH LAPORTE

Every night I close my eyes and I taste it on my breath.
　　The sweat runs into my mouth, the fear like acid burning my tongue.
Every night I grit my teeth and I smell the smoke.
　　The dust clots in my nose like a scab waiting to be ripped off.
Every night I cover my ears to make the screaming stop.
　　The children are there no matter how much I beg them to leave.
Every night is a nervous scramble, a puzzled look and nobody cares.
　　I push on towards the objective, dragging myself forward.
　　My untied boots stumble through the bricks and broken glass.
　　Why am I the only one that's trying to stop?
Every night the helicopters hover overhead and I peer into the black of
night, the endless abyss, and I wonder, "When will it end?"

NIGHT TERRORS AND PROGRESS

HART VIGES

Night terrors
And progress
Blade by the bed
lose your blood to the floor
lose my soul
That's the deal
help the dead back to the creator
takes time to get it back
fear your own hand may take your life
Blade to the closet
Don't want to scare love
bokken[1] wood grasped
Don't want to kill
Got the plan
Hide my love in the closet
close the door tight
time to hunt
check all angles
An inch can kill
All corners covered
don't breathe so loud
room by room
watch your six...it might get hot
window by window
do you see the sniper?
lock by lock
softly glide your feet
open the door with a growl
walk the perimeter with a cigarette
I take comfort in Orion but he is nowhere in sight
a knee took
a sound you make can cover the sound that kills
out your face!
My Face
My Bowl
My Love
With soft voice caressing me
a sound you make can cover the sound that kills
Don't choke your love
Don't cover her mouth

Dive blindly into the unknown
breath
unafraid
recite

I revealed myself to them in the Flesh
I found them all intoxicated
Not one of them was thirsty
And my soul grieved for the Children of Humanity
For they are blind in their hearts
They cannot see
Naked they came into this world and naked they will leave it
When they have vomited their wine
They will return to themselves[2]

push-ups...'til she gets tired
pull-ups...can't be grounded
jump rope at four in the morning
Progress and night terrors

---

[1] wooden sword (Japanese)
[2] from the Gospel of Thomas, Logion 28

ECHOES IN NOVEMBER
NICOLE GOODWIN

When Veterans Day came around
I used to tremble at the thought of it
I did this for eight years, eight years
Silently lamenting what I had been labeled
What I had been attached to.
Because no one knows the pain,
The torment, the agony
Of having seen war first hand
And till this day none of it makes sense.
It's like an open wound being stabbed by life
Daily, with no remorse
Over and over again.
I wish I could explain it better, maybe then
There would be no wars.
No chaos to frighten the world at large
It would merely be a fairy tale
One that's grim,
Used to scare little children
Once they have gotten "out of line."

NOT FEELING IT ANYMORE

RAYMOND CAMPER

I'm sorry, but I just don't feel it anymore.
I am no longer swelling up with pride when I see the Stars and Stripes,
No longer on my feet as you play 'land of the free'...

This place is still an unfulfilled promise,
Still not being honest,
Still telling us to buy into its manufactured dream...

I'm sorry, but I just don't see it anymore.
When I see basic Civil Rights tread upon,
While the corporate whoring goes on and on...

This is still a hostile place,
Still abusing the poor, the homeless, the displaced,
Still selling us lies as we are deployed far away,
Smiling with your pride-blind eyes and a handshake,
While we return as only fragments of who we used to be.

WAR TALK

NATHAN LEWIS

Sometimes we talk about nothing but the war. Sometimes we avoid it. Sometimes we are all in high spirits and enjoying ourselves. Inevitably the war is brought up. A funny story about a friend from back home will lead someone else into a similar story about one of their friends. The story will start light and soon it will descend into discomfort and personal agitation. Story begets story and the one uppers will raise the carnage meter. At this point the discussions usually break down into a poker game of sorrow. The chips are dead comrades and terrible atrocities. "I call your loss of your best friend and raise you 5 dead platoon members." An innocent story about a goofy hick friend from Georgia can lead into an unpleasant story about an IED attack and the ensuing chaos. Or maybe it will lead into a tale of a mortar attack, then capture, then smashed hand with mortar tube. Tim O'Brien was right. A true war story leaves us all silent, uncomfortable and troubled.

DEAR LION X-RAY

GARETT REPPENHAGEN

It's me again,
just checking in,
like we used to do.
From route warhorse, the JCC[1],
from Shadow Two-Two.

Remember when,
we got caught,
pinned down.
Ambushed on an infill.
In a ditch,
taking rounds.

I called for fire,
we walked mortars
up the palm tree line.
You always had my back those days.
Well, maybe not all the time.

Like when I was calling sit-reps[2],
from Hibhib[3].
When all that shit broke out.
We could have used some help back then
From my fellow Scouts.

Well, we shared some times,
the two of us,
the crazy shit we've seen.
I'll be calling in
from time to time
in a panic or in my dreams.

Maybe you can explain to me
what the hell it was all about.
Lion X-Ray, Lion X-Ray
this is Shogun-One over,
Lion X-Ray, Lion X-Ray
this is Shogun-One out.

---

[1] Joint Command Center
[2] Situation Reports
[3] small village in Northern Iraq

THE SMOKE ALSO RISES

P.W. COVINGTON

Why do the conspiratorial giggles
From teenage girls at the bookstore
Make me long for machine gun fire
And strong black tea?
What of all those precious, beloved, infants of American inheritance?
Held tighter to their mothers' chests
When they pass me on the street
And I know exactly how far the blood would flow
If I were to grab that tender package...
So unique, so special
Yet the simple mix of zygotes and lustful urges
If I were to grab it by its ankles,
And swing it, head first, into the red brick wall
Beside me,
What of it if I know exactly how far the blood would flow?
Cigarette smoke rises on the breeze from a table of
Affectedly disaffected young women
Black hair dye and nail polish
Cell phones and talk of Facebook communiqués
The Smoke Also Rises from the ruins of a minaret[1]
While golden-mocha boys in green T-shirts
Point plastic Kalashnikovs[2] at me
As they spit at the prayers of an infidel
And those damned,
Those God-damned stickers and magnets
Posted so close to car trunks stuffed fat with
Useless, plastic, holiday crap
Save the bumper stickers for your honor student
I guess a magnetic ribbon, made in China
is the next best thing to actually fighting yourself
Why do Low-impact patriotism
And carefully measured sentiment
Make me hear mortar fire and sirens
And the screams of faceless Marine riflemen?

---

[1] distinctive architectural feature of Islamic mosques, generally a tall spire
[2] Avtomat Kalashnikov is commonly used to refer to a type of rifle

DOCTOR'S AMNESIA
FREDERICK FOOTE

It can't be rare these days. After the wars,
watching Discovery Channel safe at home,
I saw a back I knew from angled mirrors:
those pinched, frenetic features were my own.
And then the blow of memory's return:
unbearable burns, charred from the waist on down,
scrubbing so fast my fingers seemed to blur,
the flesh, the cries, immediate yet far,
were all as if you saw them on TV.

I saw the things Prime Time would never see
caught by the cameraman beside the bed.
The child was just the age of my own son.

MILITARY=PRISON
CHERISH HODGE

I am mystified, attracted and moved by the power of one's energy. I find energy deeply in places I have never been and I am forever reminded by simple tunes, vibrant memories, spoken words and the temperature of air of where I have physically placed energy before.

I recall Korea as if it were a great war, forgotten graveyard and moment in time when all other things melted away leaving me and those I had to survive with alone in a position of space no one else entered. I recall this great and fearful place with harsh feelings and even pleasant memories because of the human impact and cost. Both were great; both left their mark and continue to. So was the place I would come to know well whether I liked it or not.

I left Ventura, Ca… as an ego driven, lost, confused, angry, depressed, hopeful, positive, naïve, soft little girl. I had in no way grown into any type of understanding of the world around me. No one at the age of 19 is ready for the undertaking I stepped up for. Still, we all step up on our own accord, as I did too in the beginning summer months of '03.

Just a girl… When I came back I'd be even more screwed up and unrecognizable to myself. I'd come back with so much to say and remember. I'd come back with my own maladjustments, misguided judgments, broken marriage and very damaged system. I don't know what else I was supposed to come back with. I had just gotten out of prison and prison makes for hard times and hard feelings. Still, as sure as the flowers did find reason to grow even where too much blood had been shed, I would find reasons to grow too. Into a better friend, a better daughter, a better wife and even a mother before my own time. Out of the broken pieces and very burnt ash, I had emerged with more materials to construct my own puzzle pieces out of.

This too can be said for my childhood, for my early years in marriage or early years as a mom but there's a unique flavor to military prison time. You don't just jump on your battle buddy's bed when you're bored, you jump on his body to save it both literally and not. Your hours sometimes are counted by the amount of time you spend checking in on their "mental health" or removing them from the scene of a very bad crime. Whether that crime is against themselves, humanity or another person, you learn to grab the back of the person next to you almost instinctively. There are benefits to this but those benefits were over shadowed too often.

You really did become too afraid to awaken because in those first futile moments of arousal when you can't move your arms yet, there was no telling if the alarm sounding was real or fake. It's like your genetic makeup told you that all attempts to fight would be worthless because you knew everyone was incredibly drunk or hung over and wouldn't even respond to the alarm but you still had to try despite what your molecular structure told you was best. In the responding moments before an attack, after what we were repeatedly exposed to in prison, it made more sense to laugh and sit back and wait to die then fight. That was the primal instinct constructed within us through the military.

I lost friends in prison. Lost them to the drug passed out by our command – alcohol. Lost people I didn't know and lost people I would've liked to have known. Even those that could've potentially raped me, I felt a kinship with. I felt moved and full of the life force around me because we all shared the same burden. I loved my brothers and sisters. Thank god I was never fully violated by them because the death of that family would've cost my sanity very dearly. I did love them so. Especially the new ones. The new children to be abused. We hated the same things, felt the whip the same way and could still recall what it was like on the outside. The food, the human rights, the personal dignity. We still could remember the taste of the outside whereas the old inmates could not. So we usually could not connect with our elder, more wiser, more abusive "counterparts." Maybe that was a good thing.

I tend to start these reports with enthusiasm and even happiness towards the military. But once the writing gets deeper, I tend to forget. Real feelings come out. The black and white of these pages reminds me of the black and white life we lead and how it caused too much red. I guess memories might retain their merit if left in one's head for only that tiny, believing audience to observe.

THE TOWER

IRIS M. FELICIANO

When did I lose the capacity to cry?
When my soul dried up like wells in the desert heat.
Your open wounds were flooded with tears
but my hands were not strong enough to make you live.
Now my strength has become a wall
over which you could only wave a flag to indicate your love.
A mother's hug shielded in a layer of kevlar and guilt.
A brother's send-off masked in a feast of gluttony and fear.
Sleep, only a rock and a pill away.
When did I lose the capacity to be?
Like a sculpture asked only to resemble,
to endure,
represent, stoically
the vagueness of honor.
When did I lose?

REALIZATION

TOBY HARTBARGER

sometimes the streets
seem the same as over there
sometimes the threat
is everywhere
sometimes I'm here
but I've forgotten where
sometimes I forget
to feel or even care
sometimes it's quite clear
that I died over there

DISTORTED VIEW / TOBY HARTBARGER

*"Your pain is the breaking of the shell
that encloses your understanding."*

Khalil Gibran, Lebanese-American artist

MSR TAMPA I

CONSTANTLY CHASING CATHARSIS

"I have, at last, returned to life.
I taught myself to feel by writing out
narratives of those times I remembered
becoming numb in increments,
and by reading the writings to citizens."

Ted Sexauer, Vietnam Veteran, Author
—from "Progress Report"

DOMESTICATED

ZACHARIAH DEAN

That necklace around your throat isn't jewelry; it's a rope. It's reckless when you gloat because you choke with every little note of beauty for the brooch. Boast vanity with every tug of the chain, engrossed with the insanity fitting snug around the veins, but you know true suffering and the place from which it came; a home without hugs; constantly chasing catharsis by charity from the complexity of the shame.

DIAGONAL WANDERINGS AND UPSIDES

SARAH BEINING

Only one way to go besides backwards and that is diagonal. We never go where we set out to go. I resent being the load-bearing recipient of a voice fuming righteous disappointment in which I am, as an inattentive, intelligent, preoccupied, clumsy, warm human. It is who I am.

Well. Don't attempt to "make" me feel bad for an honest mistake. Don't look at me as I have failed you in forgetting to pick up the cup. Don't huff off, offended, sad, emoting my punishment while I sweep up the ants, crawling, darkly frenzied on a cracked white dustpan only to be dumped out irreverently as I hit it against the cement garage floor. And I do it again. And I do it again. Living under your distressed conservative displeasure is enjoyable enough without the way you insist on throwing baleful sinew-balls of my inconvenient anticlimactic life as you stomp off and slam your door. Do you truly go where you think you are going, there in your room, hiding from me? Withholding my mother, year after year, shrouded by dust, talking of death? Your pain is my exquisite agony, as it were.

But when I have been at work all day, gone away, and I see that you forgot, too, and you too have allowed those black invasion mini-soldiers on six legs crawl all over an irreverent red tortilla chip on the floor, I do point it out to you, I have to say it, and I've been timidly retaliating for thirteen years. It is a peculiar tenderness when you ignore my voice, again and again, and manage to look distractedly disgusted when you finally sneer, "do you want me to pick it up?"

"No," I say, weary. "No."

Tired is just as it rests, motion leeched out by obligation, time, will, demeanor, stride, thrust, bow and trudge; I'm so, so tired here. So tired of creating the enlarged brand of my fault to create reasons for all the sharp tones, shrill gestures, blunted accusations, dogmatic resignations and crying, always crying and tears and loathing: a great big concrete bubble of pure loathing. So many tears. It would be a wonder any one stays hydrated, except for the obvious, all the drinking of bitter anger and narrow jealous eyes. The tears dry up, start building deep storage for the next shift in tactics which allow no personal responsibility to be accepted, ever, in any manner, definitely not willingly or with humility, unless we change those definitions to mean this eternally ravaged god-upon-the-rocks relationship among closely-quartered warring tribes incorrectly called "family."

Five years ago in Iraq, I wanted to stay there. It was almost relaxing. One focus, one job: I worked a 12-hour shift; I counted bodies in incident reports; I briefed the general; I analyzed attacks; I ate; I exercised; I read books; I watched television shows on DVD boxed sets and movies, too many movies to even have time to watch; and I knew mostly where I could get hurt.

Home: five, six years gone by, and my mother isn't proud of me. I do not make her happy. I don't recall her smile, except in laughter at political cartoons. I want that woman to smile at me as I smile at my young daughter, toddling about, being generally obnoxious like she is meant to be at her age; I smile at her just with love because she is perfect, even as she sticks her fingers in my eyes, pulls on my legs, refuses to be potty-trained, and screams at me to leave her alone in her finer moments. My mother does not look at me as if I am accepted because I'm her daughter. She's not proud. She's disappointed. I am not fine.

In the desert, I was good at my job. Here, my oldest brother condemns me with his religion, branding me a fornicator and sneers at my offer to use my skills in education and analysis to help him not fail out of an opportunity for a future beyond work at the local Marathon station, where he also sneers at food stamp recipients who spend "too many" food stamps on candy or energy drinks.

Fuck. I thought I was lonely in Iraq.

I was, though. I mean, so much that I did, I died, so many times there in the cloying desert air, my heart forcefully claiming a friend, reaping the affection with all my exuberance, making a family of two, clawing out from under lonely sorrow… But Zelig and I were true—he smiled; that's what I remember the most about his appearance, and he thought I was just fine, just me, sufficient. I always wanted to come home when I was in Iraq. I can't believe I wanted to leave the moment when I was worthy, come back for those ants on the floor.

Explanatory monologues abound in the tune of "of course" and "naturally," those custodians of that surface-level acknowledgement of commonly claimed human "nature." Of course, the ruminating ersatz philosopher acknowledged with a wry twisting of chipped-green-painted toes over summer-roughened feet, there had to be a common human character. Oh.

Of course, we were both twenty years old, customarily inexperienced as far as soldiers go. We were both merely two more under-aged and greener than we often dissembled, dressed as army soldiers who cared about the persons dressed as our vastly dissimilar yet corporately American parents who we could not follow, not even with all our top secret equipment and assessment and reporting and delivering. Of course, of course, of course, it was all only natural, together swallowing occupation of a sovereign nation dust in deep heaps of misgivings, that it quickly and pervasively became obvious that Zelig and I shared an articulated-without-overt-personal-peculiarities anxiety about home.

He worked the same shift as I did in Baghdad, in which we'd pass hours in a different area of the same circulated detached-air building. Weird friends, joined by a conspicuous dearth of social aptitude and ambition, we came together every few hours to smoke cigarettes in the relative sanctity of large communications vehicles and supplies. Early on, too soon, we noticed a sign on the ground that said only "Exit." The sign was strange, so apparent, lying lonely on the ground in the dirt and dust, obscured by particles and the gloomy light of the midnight shift, illuminated only by the bright stars of the

Baghdad night. We were collectively saddened by the idea it represented and truthfully couched in jokes our wish that we could somehow animate the action the sign represented and use it as a door to home, effectively making Iraq a dream or nightmare and home the reality we might wake up to.

It has been almost six years. The Exit sign gleams madly, bathing in that phony spectacle anyplace my eyes, those oblique time wanderers, glint across as two browsing diagonal sages. "All the things we've lost, we'll never have to lose them again," Cohen croons in old age sex swagger and confident existence from inadequate monitor speakers; it is during his firmly enchanting smoky-hued immutable assurances that I realize I didn't start listening to Leonard Cohen until after Iraq.

I collect miniature upsides.

MAD LONELY WORLD

JONAS LARA

as I walk along and wonder
devour demons with my bare hands
thoughts exposed for a moment
feeling lonely
with people surrounding me
feeling lonely
hey yo Jonas, it's gonna be ok
feeling lonely still
reject the drawers for the pills
taking over, expand the blood vessels
controlled thoughts no longer random
imagination held at ransom
only to exist, through terror tantrums
exists in the deepest abyss of my expression
feeling lonely
the most high is overshadowed by dark thoughts
not allowed to succeed so easily
not without struggle
try to break away hesitation, no concentration
friends look at my face and think they know where I've been
but have no idea
they think they know where I've been
they think they know what I know, where I've been
they've been thinking, they know what I know
what I think, I think that I know
where I've been, I think that I know where I've been to know why
for a moment, I'm feeling lonely

THIS IS WAR

MICHAEL DAY

I am afraid I am going to die alone who is going to want to be with me inside
my messed up head and dealing with the horrible things that I think about
myself and the world I can't stop crying and I don't know what will make
it better I am really scared that I am going to die alone I don't want money
I don't want fame I don't want a nice car or a house I just don't want to die
alone I can't even type right now I am crying so hard and I thought oh well
just let it flow and see what comes of it I am not so sure this was a good idea
it hurts so bad snot dripping from my face and my eyes flooded with tears
and I don't care I am just drooling and crying and wondering if it will end
and if it does end who will it end with they say write about what you know
and I feel like I don't know anything anymore so how can I write I am scared
I will die alone in this dumb apartment in a place where no one ever comes
and I just don't feel like I have much left in me like there is nothing left inside
I feel dead already and numb and who would want me like this and who
would like me like this and who would need me like this and I want to wake
up and everything is fine but everything is not fine and I can't sleep because
of bills and I have to work because of bills so I will get up and just go to
work and pretend that it is okay but it is not okay and I need help and I want
to check in to somewhere that can help me but the bills bills bills where will
I live I have a lease I need help but I can't not yet one more bill to pay I hate
the way we live I hate the way I live I can't figure anything out why is everything so foreign to me I know what is going on but I have no clue and that is
a horrible feeling to have deep inside you that only comes out when someone
provokes you or you've had one too many or you see that same look of pain
in a friends eyes and know exactly what they are going through but you can't
do anything because you can't even help yourself and when the hugs don't
work anymore what is left what is left what is left

NUMB

SEAN CASEY

it's unexpected and unwanted but a responsibility, resilient
I'm alone, stepping into an unknown abyss, strength
detoured from a blossoming path, hope

slipping into uniform, an unforeseen sense of confidence, comfort
building a body and mind back into its old form, determination
leading, mentoring, taking charge, self-worth

daily communication with loved ones, relaxation
two weeks to go, anticipation
trained my replacement, he's taking over, relief
holding the release paper in hand, freedom
boarding a plane for the final leg of this journey, warmth

emerging from the gate, tension
crowds applauding, embarrassment
greeted by family, blank
embraced by a loving girlfriend, empty

reunited with all that was longed for, NUMB

FROM BLACK TO RED

JON TURNER

In the neuropathic web of memories
   twilighting the shroud of confusion
In the reels upon reels of desert nomads
   dressed in black leather glasses
   amid search parties and unknown families
   seeking solitude in farm fields drained for the day
In the canopies of electrical wire suspended above
   long clay brick walls and metals doors
   humming with foot march
In the hand gestures of foreign tongue
   silently praying to live

In the scattered clothes and pictures
   spat with nicotine
   and the torn bags of grain
   weeping in warm kitchens
In the fly bitten child bundles
In the rocks you threw at us
   and the screams you cry aloud
In the urine that you drank
In the water you did not
In the patch panted and
   barefooted rug rats
In the follower
   the smiler
   the shy
In the blue eyed grins of Amreeki light
   when they see more than just monsters
   Mista mista give me pencil

In the snarling tooth of 4 am mange
   and visible ribs
In the useless abuse to found moral and
   and the tearful death of her headless body
   thrown over cement wall
In the riddled buildings seen only through
   green haze and ambient moon
In the separation of wailing mother
   and placid son
In the deformities and DU[1] dust

In the hoot and holler of
   pole breaking pills
   the over flowing glass
   the need for one more
In the alleyways of alcoholic visions

staining the damp piss ground with
   post-war song
 In the fishing line cast with two hooks in
   midday wave
In the early evening brew walking away
In the handfuls of orange bottle
   delight drowning in the sound of harp
In the red dress hallucination
   watching a little boy run circles
   with a man who spoke of
   deadened nerves
In the crying
In the knife
In the blood
   alone

In the park just down the street
   snowing over formation feet —
   bound and over watch
In the working parties slinging sandbags
   up six long flights of exhaustion
In the sand dusted water bottles
   stacked in a storm of anger
   and depression
In the burning piles of shit smothering
   the last bits of fresh air
In the very merry round ups escorting
   fancy brass through a murder pit
   of 295
In the unknown fears of when and where
   and who
In the want of running on rooftops in crackling
   hell — reloading posts with lead death
   every fifth gleams red

In the dreams of Molotov cocktails
   touching the sweet lips of
   innocent war mongers sowing their
   seed within the air conditioned ruins of Anbar
In the blistering tragedies
   of unknown skin disorders
   again and again
In the dismantling mortar blasts
   through bunk beds, sidewalls, shoulders
   faces and screams
In the explosions overwhelming the sweet
   sound of Susie's back home
In the dust clouded rooftop patios —
   broken glass, piss bottles and cigarette butts
In the unprotected catnaps through 130 degrees
In the instantaneous awake from distant thump
   and the unknowing

In the lies to my mother
  "I'm ok"
In the lies to my peers
  "I'm ok"
In the lies to myself
  "I'm ok"
In the first time chest nuzzle
In the maple tree out front
In the long planned celebrations
  ending in drunken face slaps
  and cum
In the confusion of families
  the slamming of doors
  the hurried shuffles
  the silence and stares
In the urge to go back

In the wife
In the husband
In the perfect baby
  and dog
In the weight of hearts five years past

In the reasons for sobriety —
  lashing out with callused fists
  from beating the mindless numb
In the same stores overly thought of
  and never talked about or those talked
  too much of
In the space headed stares and not knowing
  what time is arrival
  he   she is back there
In the depressions
  the fears
  the rage
  the thoughts
  the full body drains

In the acceptance of disaster as a
  balancing medium for all shaping's
  of peace
In the crystals washed over repeatedly
  with sand, smoke and sun in the
  stranglehold of Poseidon's breath
In the feathered prayers and medicines
  made with sacred thought

In the unwritten letters and poems —
  are the hidden faces of war

---

[1] Depleted Uranium

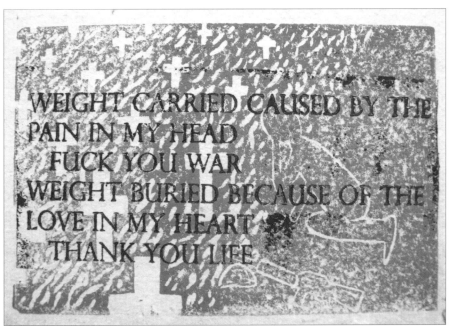

UNTITLED (COMBAT PAPER) / JON TURNER

PRAYER BOOTS / JON TURNER

PTSD

CHANTELLE BATEMAN

sadness is the color of my eyes, of my heart
the same shade as distance
and some kind of Miles Davis on repeat
it's the sound I don't want anyone to hear
creeping out of my pillows in the morning
before the coffee and cigarettes begin
an avatar when I'd rather just be myself

my anxiety smells like teen spirit
and whatever it is that makes mean dogs bare their teeth
it sounds like trees falling, like doors slamming
like a pin drop sometimes
like my mother checking on me...AGAIN
and feels like nothing
absolutely FUCKING NOTHING

anger is the color I sometimes paint the town with
bright red, blood shot, and sparkling with tiny salt crystals
louder than incoming and the sirens they play when I hit the deck
bitter sweet and never offered cookies
I'm just a pile of tears needing to punch you

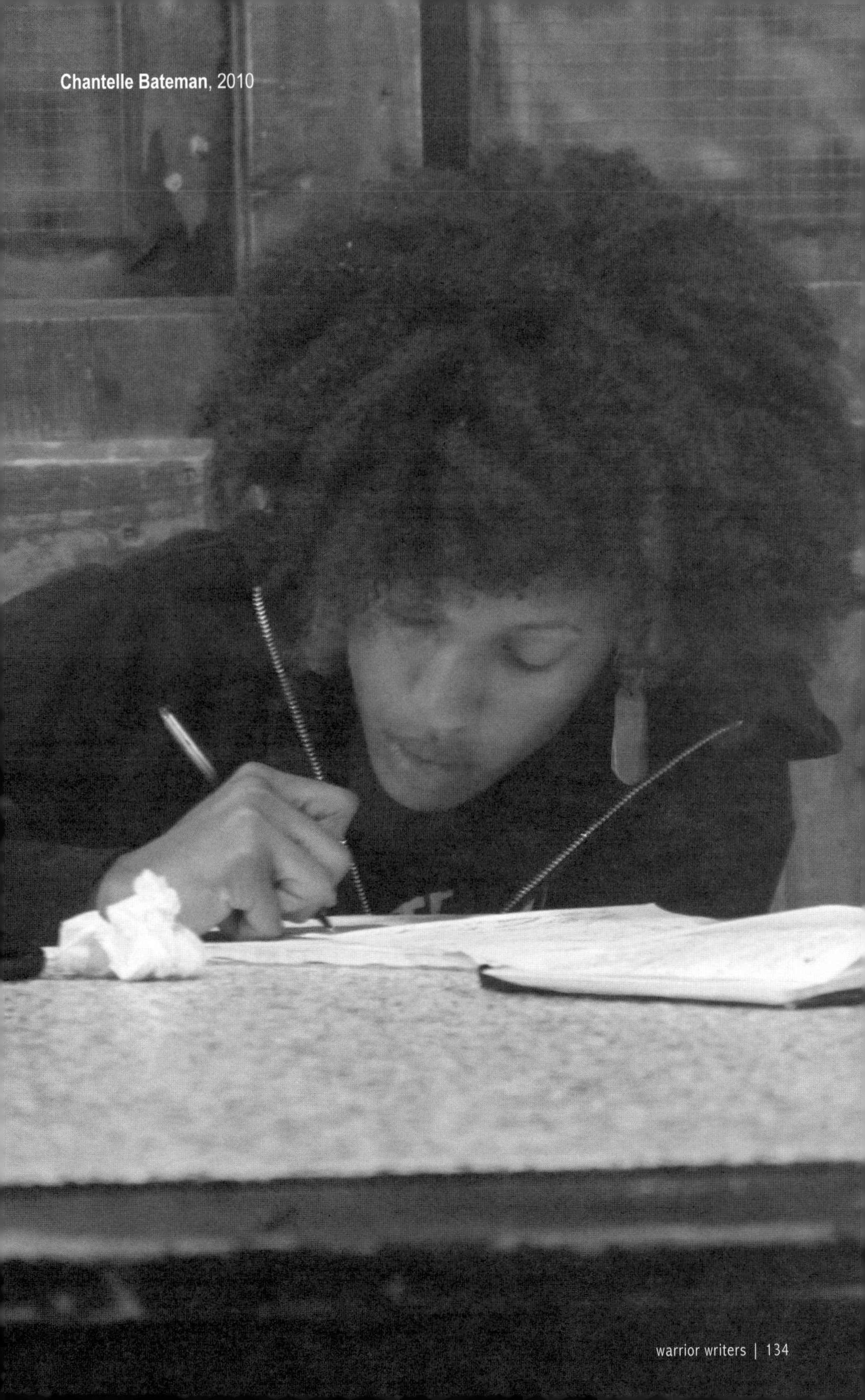

Chantelle Bateman, 2010

WINTER SOLDIER

KEVIN KILGORE

WINTER SOLDIER / KEVIN KILGORE

SCARS

JOSIAH WHITE

The bomb went off just down and opposite the road where he momentarily stood, facing outward, rifle clutched half-heartedly, waiting for the enemy he knew would never come running over the ridge. Shrapnel struck liberally over the left side of his body. Whoever made the bomb must have been proud of the spread and devastation. He had dropped instantly and the searing pain in his limbs and face kept him from standing back up. His hands, now free of his weapon, clawed outward reaching for a respite. Nothing went through his mind. Not the proper order of first aid, nor the three types of bleeding: venous, capillary, and arterial, nor the fact that he had all three. The hours spent in classes meant nothing to him. They had no way of grounding him to this universe as the blood trickling over his clenched eyelids filtered the already diffuse yellow light into a pallid crimson darkness.

He was vaguely aware of pounding feet, jostling, rending of fabric, a metallic taste, and a deep pinprick. Then he slept.

Weeks after returning to America and days after walking without the use of crutches, he was allowed a temporary return to civilian life. His parents rolled out a bag full of trinkets he had collected from the generals and important people who visited the hospital. In his pocket he kept the purple medal they had pinned on him while he lay in bed with the opiates coursing through his veins. Another paper bag held two rattling yellow bottles; two pills every four hours and one in times of extreme pain. Tucked deep away were rolls of gauze, white tape, and moist pads for direct placement on open wounds. The head nurse made him and his parents promise to change his last four bandages at least once a day and twice, if the discharge was heavy enough. He had seen so many nurses and orderlies working over him and cleaning up his once uncontrollable defecation in the confusing days after the explosion, then later with deft hands snipping at black threads criss-crossing his skin, that he jokingly said he could be a registered nurse. In reality he never wanted to see the underside of human skin ever again.

The two weeks elapsed with much of it spent in front of the television, watching without thinking until visions of his war flashed before his eyes forcing him to mash the off button. One night he went to dinner and a movie with a few of his high school friends. They were happy to see him again and hugged him lightly, minding the noticeable bandages. They asked questions like How was it over there? They treating you all right? Without ever asking the one they all wondered: Why did you go over there? Once the important parts of his story were told and all of the easily digestible and non-gory anecdotes exhausted, the conversation turned towards former classmates and their goings-on. He laughed when required, nodded to the beat of the conversation, stared into nothing during the silences, and fulfilled his social duty without ever exposing the turmoil underlying his conscious thought. During the movie, protected by darkness and singular field of vision, a few tears leaked out before he silenced them with a white pill flushed down with soda.

Every morning and night he surveyed the newly painted canvas of his body; the pits, furrows, splotches, which, only a few months ago, stood out in his mind's eye as signs of bravery and virility. Now he was hesitant to extend his left arm and leg as the taut skin disturbed sensitive nerves, sending out alien shocks the like of which healthy bodies never experience. With quivering hands he sought out his face's newly defining features: two perfectly rectangular bandages, one running from cheekbone to nose, the other from mid-jaw to chin, under which lay the oozing horror of his existence. He knew one day they would heal and he could no longer cover them from inquisitive eyes. From now until death, eyes will be drawn away from his blue eyes to two thick jagged lines running parallel across his face. No amount of plastic surgery, sunglasses, or baseball caps will ever truly erase the result of a brief moment of time — milliseconds — the culmination of a series of ill-thought decisions by himself and others.

At the end of the two weeks his parents left him to limp slowly towards the airplane that would spirit him back to the hospital and military life. He still had some recovery ahead and a few cosmetic procedures to endure, but one day he would be discharged and would have to make real decisions about his life. He contemplated his future and the role he would assume. Would he retain the warrior spirit which had already etched its signature upon his surface, or would he reject it and grasp outward into a world and philosophy foreign to him, of which he could never interact without the scars of body and spirit forcefully altering the way he is perceived?

VETERAN

JAMES A. MOAD II

Born of war and the lie of lies, buried and uniformed into silence,
signed away lives in pursuit of *Service*
commanding you to hold onto some flag or book
that clings to *Patriotism* as if it's a guiding star
leading us to a future of promises and certainty
until coming home breaks itself upon you in a wave you can't see —
an invisible bomb blast, and there's the *Duty* to be back,
to be right, to be a person who can forget,
while the day drives a memory back into light,
into a war that won't let you go —
won't allow you to escape the world of *Honor* you're supposed to hold high
like a *Flag* hoisted on the moon, showing you what we once could do,
but you can never *Reconcile* the day with the night —
the ghosts in the mind — the holes in the thoughts,
until they tell you it's *PTSD*[1], and you listen and you hear
and you see it in the eyes of the mirror,
everything lettered into a name for what only
you and those like you can know,
men and women searching for a healing world and voice —
a gentle guide into every night's desperate end
where you find yourself over and over again
staring into darkness and pain, secrets and boxed up tears
waiting for the everything in the world to die.

---

[1] Post Traumatic Stress Disorder

☣ REDUCE(D) ☣

"YOU GO TO WAR WITH THE ARMY
YOU HAVE...NOT THE ARMY YOU
MIGHT WANT OR WISH TO HAVE
AT A LATER TIME."

- DONALD RUMSFELD DEC. '04

☣ REUSE(D) ☣

☣ RECYCLE(D) ☣

Go	No Go	US MILITARY SUMMARY
	✓	CARE FOR VETERANS
	✓	CARE FOR MILITARY FAMILIES
	✓	CARE FOR SOLDIERS WITH MST
	✓	1 IN 3 SERVICEWOMEN ARE RAPED
	✓	CARE FOR VETERANS WITH TBI
	✓	CARE FOR VETERANS WITH PTSD
	✓	# OF SUICIDES OUTNUMBER CASUALTIES
	✓	Operational Risk Assessment

REDUCED, REUSED, RECYCLED / BRYAN REINHOLDT

WE ARE BROKEN BOTTLES

MALACHI MUNCY

Reflected florescence
Refracted condescends
Nuance of neons
Outshining ions
Broken bottles
Glisten in the gutter

There is more glass in the streets here
than stars in the sky
More light in liquor stores
than shining in eyes

The bottoms of bulbs and bowls burn
brightly in front of our face
Outshining the hell we live in
as hell is outshining space

Reflected florescence
Refracted condesents
Nuance of neons
Outshining ions
Broken bottles
Glisten in the gutter

Fueled by pharmaceuticals
pill bottle bottoms bomb us
But other people's pills
are other people's problems

Even after emptying every vexing vessel to maintain
memories mixing menacing most minds may contain
Because this is a military town
there is no such thing as sane

Reflected florescence
Refracted condescents
Nuance of neons
Outshining ions
WE are broken bottles
and the might of the military is reflected in our remains.

TRAPPED / MALACHI MUNCY

THERAPY
KYLE WESELOWSKI

In this town therapy is secondary
To the needs of our cities' health and humanity
The powers that decide our livelihood make another primary priority
Deciding to fill up our bathroom cabinets instead of giving us therapy

It's all good
They like to prescribe medication to GIs
It's easier to control them when they've made them dependent on a
drug forming habit
Forget about fixing combat stress
Just hop us up on benzodiazepines
So we forget the past
Dulling our painful reality
Of what war does to our mentality
For some of us we may not have scars or limbs lost
It's taboo in this town
We all know war affects every soldier not just physically
For the pill popping soldier

Fort Hood makes it easier for us who suffer from over-medication
A normality in our health care society
Don't worry about it
If you get the shakes there's a new expressway lane for your quick fix
It just opened up for business
Roll up in your ride to Thomas Moore clinic
10 mikes later you got your fill of dependency
All that's left to do is grab a bottle of water to swallow down handicapped
half-assed therapy
So quick so easy, you'll make it back in time to your motor pool duties
The military clearly would rather find their own quick fix to the mental health
epidemic
Where did the battle buddy system go?
Anyone can be your battle buddy even General Campbell
It doesn't exist anymore
A soldier is no better than an Afghan or Iraqi
Put their problems to the side and worry about it years later after they forgot about us
Pills have their place but without therapy the veterans can't live this way forever

For many the help won't come
Suicides happen in regularity
If they're lucky they will at least see the pearly gates
The gates that big book we all know talks about

PTSD
(P.lease T.ry S.omething D.ifferent)
JEREMY STAINTHORP BERGGREN

It's not like it used to be
Not like it used to be
He said, c'mon suck it up
They said, it's time you just moved on
She said, wherever you go, there you are
And all I heard was
Nagging voices
Barking orders
Missile raids
In my head
I mean,
It's not like it used to be
You see me here, but I'm so far gone
See me here, but I'm so far gone
He said, you can make a career out of this
They said, thanks for your service, but they never ever listened
She said, you have PTSD
Post
Traumatic
Stress
Disorder
But can you
Please
Try
Seeing
Death
And then have nothing go wrong
Because you
People
Triggered a
Social
Disease
Because you don't hear shit
After we come home
Not like it used to be,
She said, you have PTSD
Post
Terror
Soul
Disorder

Passively
Timid
Sometimes
Dangerous
Pathetically
Trying
Slowly
Dying
Potentially
Terminal
Spiritual
Disease
I mean, what if I said
Fuck your
Stupid cliches, about picking yourself up
Off the god damned ground
Or letting go of the past, or
Wherever you go, there you are
What if I said
Fuck you
America
You're the disorder
Your greed, your selfishness, your lies
& what if I said
Please be forewarned
I'll be emotionally detached
When you need me the most
I'll be present but gone
& silently celebrating each slow breath
Knowing they bring me one step closer to death
& what if I said
I cannot love you, because I
Cannot love myself
What if I said
I'll just stop talking
For months,
Because I may as well be dead
& what if I said
The only reason I can make art or write with a passion is because I can hate
My paper
My pen
My self
& relationships gone like
Rounds down range
Self confidence lost like
Missing in Action
Simply struggling to move forward
No traction

Spinning.
Spinning.
Spinning.
Out of control
Won't you
Please
Try
Something
Different
Fuck your judgement, your excuses
Won't you
Please
Try
Something
Different
Fuck your pills, your prescriptions
Won't you
Please
Try
Something
Different
Fuck your meaningless, good, intentions
Won't you
Please
Try
Something
Different
I mean, just give me
A set of ears to finally hear
My truth
And shoulders to cry on when I finally
Break down
Just give me
A yoga mat and some good
Fucking weed
A war that hasn't started
A country without greed
Just
Please Try Something Different
& maybe I'll get some hope back,
Because I'm stuck in a hell
Of hopelessness
& maybe I'll stop scanning rooms
& environments & just rest
Maybe I'll stop judging myself
& just accept me for me
I mean, fuck,
She said I have PTSD

& that I had problems with trauma
Before the marines
Couldn't differentiate between
Childhood abuse
And war's excuse
Of freedom, of home
Like pain is weakness leaving the body,
Unless it doesn't leave so you just leave your body
Suicidal thoughts
Maybe became habitual
& cadenced, like
Left, right, left, right
But what's left when you finally come home
Nothing's right
& nobody knows
That anything is wrong.

Please.
Try.
Something.
Different.

STRANGE FRUIT

JEREMY STAINTHORP BERGGREN

MY DAY
GEOFF MILLARD

Fuck! The alarm.

Eyes still closed, I try throwing my arm across my body and across the bed, aiming for the snooze button, but I'm too stiff and pain shoots from my back to my toes. Pain so bad it takes my breath.

Second try...YES, I got it! Ten minutes to stretch and figure a way to take my first pills.

1 Oxycodone for pain

1 Cyclobenzaprine to loosen the rocks that are my back muscles

1 Omeprazole for heartburn and stomach pains

1 Docusate to help soften my stool (little side effect of the Oxycodone)

1 Gabapentin to ease the pain from the nerves pinched in my back. The pinched nerves mainly are the same that control my left testicle, making it feel as though someone has my left nut in a vise.

FUCK! Alarm again. This time I get the off button.

Sitting up, I know right away my pain level is at 7 out of 10. With the VA[1] always asking what my level is, it's become second nature to be always calculating.

My feet hit the floor. Rolling my shoulders, I stand, using the wall to steady myself. I creep slowly to the kitchen for some cereal. The dog runs for her bowl too. I'm glad for the basement apartment with no stairs, but the dog will need to go out. I crack the door and she runs.

I flop down in my chair, flip on the morning news, hoping not to hear the names of anyone I know who may have been killed in Iraq, yet somehow hoping that maybe today will be the day the news talks about my war. Once again, it's not mentioned, so I eat my Cheerios. Ready for the next pill.

1 Diclofenac for the inflammation of both my knees and back.

The shower feels so good as I stretch under the hot water. Brushing my teeth and — ahhh, motherfucker — the mouthwash burns my cheeks from last night's bite marks. The docs say I have TMJ, whatever that means.

Shit...I'm late, toss on clothes running to work. I catch a bumpy thirty-minute bus ride, returning my pain level to 6.

1 more Oxycodone and its mate, Cyclobenzaprine, for the muscle spasms that are now shooting pain down my legs. Walking into the building for work, I'm bent over from what feels like a kick to the balls. Another Gabapentin.

Work is, well...work. I can't sit for more than thirty minutes, nor stand for more than ten. I must look twitchy to my coworkers. Another Diclofenac for inflammation, but crap, too soon before lunch...Heartburn. Now I need some Tums.

Lunch is a meal on the go because work does not care that my pain level is back to a 7. I can feel a migraine coming, so I down 2 Sumatriptan Succinate with a Red Bull for kick.

I used to be an athlete before Iraq. Now I'm overweight and struggle to walk on the elliptical machine for twenty minutes.

Pain is at an 8 now, so I pop the third Oxycodone of the day, followed by none other than its pal Cyclobenzaprine. I limp onto the bus, putting as much weight as I can onto my cane, and head home for dinner where I take my third Diclofenac. After I eat, this time.

I hang my cane by the door and roll my wrist to sooth its aching. Just another side effect. I rub some Trixaicin on my back before I watch the news with ice packs on my knees.

On a great night I'll have someone over and sex could ensue, but I have to make sure that an hour before, I pop a Verdebafil to counteract the boner-killing side effects of the Cyclobenzaprine.

Getting ready for bed means my nighttime cocktail: 3 Nortriptyline for pain, migraines, and to help me sleep. They are also antidepressants, but don't work for that at all. Also the last 2 Gabapentin for the night.

As I lie down, my back sharply contracts, forcing me to yelp and grimace. I stay as still as I can until things loosen up some. The pain is unbearable. I stick the pads from my Tens unit on my lower back the best I can, but they never seem to be totally right. The electricity hurts at first, but soon helps fatigue the muscles enough to loosen them.

After my back calms, I can feel my knees shooting with pain all their own. I rub some 5% Lidocaine ointment over them to take the edge off.

An hour later, the pills start to kick in and I close my eyes hoping for rest.

Yet as soon as the world goes blank behind my eyelids I hear screams, friends dead, dying, radio crackle still distorts David's voice. I turn up my iPod to drown him out.

Just as I fade away, my stomach wakes me with a bit of nausea.

Screaming, I wake up, unsure not only of the time, but of where I am. Even in the dark I can see 9 bottles of pills across the room and debate taking all of them. If it wouldn't hurt so much to get out of bed, I might do it. Anything to just be rid of the pain!

I fade back off...

The alarm rings. Here we go again.

How will I do this for the next 30-40 years?

---

[1] Veteran Administration

WE ARE NOT YOUR HEROES

JENNIFER PACANOWSKI

We are not your heroes.
Heroes come back in body bags and caskets.

We are now society's burden,
ALCOHOLICS
DRUG ADDICTS
POTHEADS
CRIPPLES

We are displaying our pain.
Begging for help that falls onto the VA's deaf ears.
Pill popping to silence us into numbness and dead eyes.

We are not your heroes
We are now a mental disease.
NO VACCINATIONS FOR PTSD.
NO CURE for post traumatic stress disorder.
We fight for our cure with our
ALCOHOLISM
DRUG ADDICTIONS
SMOKING WEED. . .
We are hurting ourselves,
Letting society watch our pain and suffering.

WE ARE NOT YOUR HEROES.
We are your BURDEN
Smacking you in the face with our honesty of this needless war, WE FOUGHT
So you have the freedom to judge us.

I wish I never came back.

WHERE DID THE MUSIC GO?

NICK MORGAN

Where did the music go,
And why did it stop?
I can remember a time
Not far in the past
When the words made sense
And our feet tapped to the beat
Of the music so clear and pure

Where did the music go,
And why did it stop?
Amidst the clang of shells
Hitting the ground while
Piling up so very high
On a twin sized bed
That perfectly fits two

Where did the music go,
And why did it stop?
Inside a horse's head
A patch or a weapon, you choose
Lock myself safely inside
I can still hear the music
But I cannot hear the words

Where did the music go,
And why did it stop?
The words just won't come out
Just like silent sitting
Sedated in fresh morning light
I can still hear the music
Now it is silent breaking noise
That fades away daily
Like this son in the west

REFLECTING ON FIVE YEARS OF SERVICE

JESSE MICHAEL-GERONIMO VALENCIA

Reflecting on five years of service
I, now bearded and free
Do not regret anything
And yet, with some measure of sorrow
I say farewell to that daft imperial army
To state-sponsored terrorism
To blind nationalist devotion
To squeaky-clean-shaven-square-slack-jawed ignorance
I did my time and now wish to forget I ever committed myself to it
I could burn my uniforms, commit the ashes to the desert
To join the dust and snakes and filth
I no longer have to wear the threads of that ilk
No more boots, no more patches, no more rank
And out here among the people there is no rank, and rightly so
There was never a rank that was justified among the people
And I count not one of those persons my superior
They are all my equal, for I have transcended far beyond the vocabulary of war
Far past entitlement and exception, fascist mind control, conformity,
propaganda
Industry of death and wicked machinery
All manner of empty sacrifice, of blood and fire and oil
I will not support these troops, for I cannot
I will not salute this flag, for I cannot
I will not vote for these miscreants and thieves!
The symbols of our great country have been corrupted and worn.
But O, how I love thee, America
And wish that you could return to your once true glory
But all you have left for us are lamentations
Weeping and gnashing of teeth
Because your 'army of one' is truly an army of jokers and fools
Led to believe that they are fighting just wars
To ensure the freedoms of this land
When the only freedoms they are defending
Are the freedoms to imprison, to starve
To isolate and conform and the freedom to consume.

I am glad that my time has ended with them
And so, to the Army and all it stands for...
I say farewell and adieu
And good riddance.

THREE WEEKS IN

STEPHEN COVELL

I do not know if art imitates life or the reverse. Once exposed to an idea presented to you by an author or director, that experience becomes part of your consciousness. An image becomes a memory, a memory a series of images; clips that loop indefinitely, sparked by a smell or a sound. I walk down a road, rifle slung over one shoulder, right hand on the grip as it swings by my leg. The sky is the sky, but dirtier. The pavement is the pavement, but grittier. The mud is mud, but when it grabs hold it never lets go.

My eyes are now my camera, panning back and forth, filming the first cut of the movie that has become my life. That is how it feels to be back here. It is your life, but it is two dimensional, a caricature, exaggerated but familiar. It's you but there's always something missing. Something you left in a box back home, stuffed inside a dark storage unit with your clothes and your pictures. You taped down the cardboard flaps and wrote do not open for one year. You know it's a defense mechanism but you find comfort in the routine. Get up, work, eat, go to the gym, shower, eat, and repeat. It's a little like what you imagine prison to be. You see so many parallels between you and the inmates that it makes you a little angry. Angry already? It's only been three weeks. Weren't you just here a year ago? Why does it smell exactly the same? Like burning garbage and dust. Why does it feel like such a waste of time? Because from this road you can't see anything but the next step, and like the pawn, you just keep moving forward.

In the distance there are gunshots. Sometimes they are close enough to give you that familiar jolt of adrenaline that you try to pretend you have not missed. As you walk around your new home you see signs of violence and you hear the stories; the lob-bomb attacks back in March, the Green Beans coffee trailer burning down, and how we set up offices in the building they dropped a JDAM[1] on during the invasion. It is the biggest building on the FOB[2] and it has a hole in the middle of it like God put his fist through the roof. It used to be the Defense Ministry building and you hear they used to interrogate people and then toss them out the top floor windows. Now it is a gutted sagging hulk. An early victim of the shock and awe.

A few buildings over, there is a small square jail with an open inner court yard. The windows of the guard towers at each corner have long since been broken and sections are cordoned off with C-wire[3] because they are structurally unsound. They say there are Chinese characters written on the walls inside and left there by slave laborers, who were brought in to build the surrounding compound. Saddam threw a banquet for them when the buildings were completed and then had them all executed. They say a lot of things.

It gets late and even though you have worked a full day you find it hard to sleep. It is a bit cramped and the walls are paper thin. Literally, parts of them are made of cardboard. Nothing you have not been through before.

A sheet strung up for privacy and you are set. Your own little section of the world built to ward off casual intrusion. Still you cannot sleep, so you write. Send it off, maybe people read it. Some must because they write you back and it feels good to know you're being thought about. But still you sometimes wonder if you made the right choice.

Usually you come back around to the same conclusion you always do when you have too much time on your hands. You did this because you were getting lazy and complacent and you have never learned anything if it was not the hardest way you could possibly subject yourself to. And what is worse than making the wrong choice? Making no choice at all.

---

[1] Joint Direct Attack Munitions
[2] Forward Operating Base
[3] Concertina wire

ESCAPE / MALACHI MUNCY

PTSD
JON TURNER

With the fibers torn
   are memories of gun battle
   where bullets
     scream Allah
   and the deafening
     song of explosions
       dance
       where human flesh once stood
There have been nightmares
   that had made more sense
     but when dreams are reality
     clarity is non apparent
   and the gunpowder
     sacred to our veins
     is by all means the means of expression
when true meaning is burnt crisp
     and the screams fending for themselves
     are still alone
       in the desert

LYNN ESTOMIN

Jon Turner performs in Philadelphia, 2010.

CHANGE
AMBER STONE

They say change is good, but I guess it really depends on who you talk to. Sit a spell, and visit with me—just wait, listen, you'll see; how important, yet disappointing change can be. Change can make you smile, laugh, live, love, cry. It can also show you just how ugly your soul can be. Mirrors hang on my walls—I want to break them all with rocks—big rocks, like the ones you find near mountains, and speaking of mountains; how many have you climbed just to see the sun rise early in the morning, or it set so early in the winter when it's cold, bitter, ugly. Do you see what I see? Change is constantly happening... happening to you... happening to me as you hear my rants and rambling. It never stops, if just in my head, the never-ending cycle of PTSD. Like a hamster on a wheel—I go faster with this little parody. One day you feel joy, the next is so, so empty. Empty of thoughts that contribute to healing. Suicide, anger, total anxiety. They keep giving me pills to stop this war inside of me—pills may help you sleep, but the nightmares still come screaming, tossing and turning, non-stop sweating. "Will it always be like this?" I remember asking Jim, a 'Nam Vet who has been watching for all the warning signs that keep me from ever changing.

Above, Amber Stone works on her poem, "Change," during a writing workshop. **Right**, Amber Stone at the Veterans and Community Conference in Philadelphia, Pennsylvania, 2010.

Burlington, VT 2007

SOWING COMMUNITY

"In the setting sun
rests tranquility for tomorrow
rising   peace   prevails

and all chains become
broken   shattered   gone"

Jon Turner, Iraq Veteran, Warrior Writer
—from "Long Time Along"

A HAND ON THE RUDDER

LIAM MADDEN

Three years ago, I drafted a letter to Senator Obama after IVAW's dramatic showdown with two hundred riot cops at the 2008 Democratic National Convention in Denver. Our courage and reason were rewarded when Obama's advisors agreed to a meeting with us. They eventually blew it off. The momentum dissipated and our lost opportunity vacuumed the wind from my sail. Stagnant and lost, I began to explore new passages to the beckoning place in my heart.

Activism in the form represented by this "anti-war" protest letter was an island where I stopped, nourished myself and found guidance on my journey to a more whole version of myself. I mean activism that "fights the good fight," but is so ineffectual that it sucks the magic out of life. All the beauty and fun of creating something beautiful was suffocated by the need to fight, to oppose…to be against. That activism was all sail and map, but no rudder. I lacked the ability to change the course of my life based on what felt good to me. Life became a sacrifice for a good cause instead of the creation process that I intuitively knew it should be.

After the letter's failure I searched for a path my heart could say yes to. I discovered the wisdom of Buckminster Fuller who said, "You never change things by fighting against the existing reality. To change something, build a new model that makes the existing model obsolete." No quote had ever resonated so deeply. I began to piece together what later seemed obvious, that the greatest contribution I could make would be something that was new, difficult to articulate at first, but felt extremely good to pursue. My heart became my rudder and sensitivity to it became my discipline.

Three years later, I look at cities across the world hosting camps of disillusioned protesters gathering to voice frustration about our failing economy and I see a bigger victory to be had. While the "anti-war" was a noble effort, it was still merely a symptom of the whole construct, the self-cannibalizing, world-devouring, beauty-less, unfulfilling and cruel myth we have been cast in. The myth that tells us that we can trust the market to rescue our ecology from the teeth of the fossil fuel machine. The myth whose heroes wake up every morning to shackle themselves to repetitive motions of separated, money-insulated lives. The myth that uses technology-provided leisure time like a carrot dangling always out of reach.

I am excited that the myth itself is under question. Finally, "Life As We Know It" is being scrutinized. The war was my passion, so black and white, so blatantly inhumane, but even it was far too narrow to change the paradigm. Had we won, had the war ended on our terms, the dynamic that produced it would have lingered, awaiting the next exploitable opportunity. The erupting of consciousness from Tunisia to Wall Street reflects, to me, our spiritual immune system finally reacting to the systemic sickness of being separate from each other, from nature and reinforcing that separateness with the hypnotizing, distracting and consuming spell of money.

I am excited to have a hand on my rudder this time. But I am grateful for the time on the island that showed me I needed more than sails and maps.

I AM FREE / RACHEL McNEILL

A CITY BREATH
MICHAEL DAY

I walk the streets of the City, appalled at the rampant consumerism, but consuming nonetheless. My consumption, however, is not of a materialistic nature. I consume the lights, I consume the words, both unknown dialects and known dialects alike. I consume the movements of the masses and consume their immobility in the same manner.

Everything that I have learned about my Disorder leads me to believe that this is not the city for me. The noise, the movements, and the ominous intensity of the density cloud my perception. I am hyper vigilant in my consumption. I attempt to be aware of all but concentrate on none. I feel it in my movements and see my awkwardness through the facial expressions of random patrons. It is odd to think that I am but a microcosm of the momentum of the City. I am a small grain of sand in the hourglass, separate and unique among the other grains, but part of a group all heading in one direction. When I am not consuming the City I lay my head to rest on a cheap pillow on a cheap bed which rests on cheap wood inside a cheaply painted room with an expensive price tag.

"Escuchela...la ciudad respirando..." resounds from my room into the valley of buildings. I listen and I CAN feel it. I can feel the City breathing. I escape to my fire escape. I hang my feet over the edge and listen to the sounds of the City. The projects are lit up. The lights of a police helicopter rest heavy against the few spots of darkness. If you squint your eyes...I mean just barely keep them open...it looks like the lights emanating from the projects are the nerves of the City. The lights become little synapses firing, connecting all the buildings to one another to create one massive electrical charge. The City hums with a cyclic rhythm, inhaling and exhaling.

This City is alive, but it has not eaten me yet. I have weathered the storm. Perhaps it is because I saw less than is needed for my mind to fracture, as it has with so many of my fellow brothers and sisters. Regardless, I am here. I am present in this moment, one with the City. My light emanating from my room is a synapse firing to someone looking across the way from the projects. I am part of the perpetual cycle and acknowledging such calms me.

She knocks on my door and I breathe slowly. We snuck onto the roof from the sixth floor. The girl from nowhere and I, with a bottle of wine and blanket in hand we laid on the roof, connecting the stars to our imaginations and realizing from the distant project gunfire that, for some of us, bullets shatter space before they shatter minds. We breathed air easily in our own space and then drew upon one another's breaths.

I twist the dial and the sweet sound of an Edward Sharpe and the Magnificent Zeros reminds me that "home" is indeed where I am with her, although not her specifically—just "her." Suddenly far removed from the roof I am standing as a ghost behind the thoughts of a Marina Abramovic performance... "without the audience the world doesn't exist. It doesn't have any meaning." We must be present. We are that audience. Our lives are a performance. Moments are strung together to create the final act. Within the collaboration of those moments is a place called home. A home where we are present. The girl from nowhere leaves and it feels good to be good with that.

My place is a place where, without a question, I am aware of my awareness. I am present. My thoughts, my movements, my actions, and my inactions are separated from the whole. I am not one apart. I am one within. I am present in every conceivable way in my place. The City breathes for me as I breathe for it.

WORK THE ANGLES / MICHAEL DAY

SUPPORT THE TROOPS

JACOB GEORGE

"we just Need to support the troops"
is what they tell me

well, this is from a troop
so listen carefully

what we Need are teachers who understand the history of this country
what we Need is a decent living wage, so people ain't cold and hungry
what we Need is bicycle infrastructure spanning this beauteous nation
what we Need are more trees and less play stations
what we Need is a justice system that seeks the truth
what we Need are more books and less boots

what we Need is love

for every woman and man
from southern Louisiana
to the mountains of Afghanistan

Now, it's true
The troops need support
the support to come home
they need treatment and jobs
and love for the soul

see,
war ain't no good
for the human condition
I lost a piece of who I was
on every single mission
and I'm tellin' you,
don't thank me for what I've done

give me a big hug
and let me know
we're not gonna let this happen again
because we support the troops
and we're gonna bring these wars to an end

REHUMANIZATION

PETER SULLIVAN

I created this piece using what I prefer to call Service Paper since I am not a combat veteran. I used one of my old military uniforms to make the paper, then I hand-cut it using an Xacto knife.

I spent 12 years wearing a military uniform and feel that most of that time was spent learning how to kill and hate other people for reasons I am still struggling to understand. Throughout this process of dehumanization of the "enemy," I think I also learned to dehumanize myself. This piece is an attempt to begin the process of returning, not only from the place in myself that said it was OK to view others as less than human, but from the place in myself that said I was OK with doing that. Having dehumanized myself and others, I am now trying to rehumanize myself and others.

With that in mind, I chose to use the simplest expression of love I could think of and repeat it, in my own handwriting, across 12 lines on a sheet of paper. Each line represents one year of military service. I want people who view the piece to see themselves reflected in the mirror, so they will know that I am speaking directly to them, and also to have an image of themselves in front of them as they read the words, "I love you" over and over and realize that they are worthy of their own love.

COMBAT PAPER

JEREMY STAINTHORP BERGGREN

We immediately put our heads down and sort of nodded in silence. She leaned over to me and said quietly "it amazes me the courage you all have but when this happens you all shut down." She always carried a lot of our weight and cared very deeply about every single one of us.

Earlier that day I had arrived after driving a few hours to catch the last day of the workshop. I brought my uniforms upstairs to the studio and placed them on a table.

He came over to me and spoke softly, asking me if I had done this before. I hadn't. He got me started by telling me to remove all the buttons, any medal—like my rank insignia or awards, my nametapes, and boot ties. I cut my uniforms into small strips, about an inch wide by a couple inches long. It took a while and more of my friends were arriving. This was the last batch at this workshop and I was anxious to get some of my uniforms in, to see what it would feel like. Even though I had conversations in the studio while I was cutting my cammies[1] up I mostly remember thinking:

About that time staff sergeant Blankenship had got in my car to ride to the burial with me, because he knew I wasn't okay driving alone.

About the stories my friends had told me—finding that soldier that had shot himself through the head with his rifle in the port-a-potty on that base in Iraq—but he was in there like eight hours before they got him—he was just cooking in there above the shit.

About that time I started singing the Chili's song in the morgue when we saw that burned body—and Charlie chiming in.

About all these moments that were scattered around my head and were still bouncing around but I was just trying to make sense of it all.

When I finished I had a pile of cammies all cut up next to a small pile of buttons, my ranks, nametapes, and boot ties. That rank and my nametapes is what distinguished me from other Marines and it was so small compared to the pile of shredded uniforms in front of me.

My uniforms were put into the last batch to make paper—it's placed in a trough with a machine that spins it around, cutting it up and pulping it into mush. When it is the right consistency it is placed into 5-gallon buckets with more water. The pulping, pulling the paper, and drying all took place outside. It was a cool day in May above the city right by the lake. It was cool, but sunny, and the wind was coming off the lake. I remember looking at those 5-gallon buckets at that mush of uniforms...what once was a uniform, now about to get turned into paper. It looked like porridge or split pea soup. Like you could eat it.

We took turns pulling—that's where you take the pulp and put it into a bin with water and pull it with a screen, sifting out the water until the pulp is a

COMBAT PAPER CHICAGO / JEREMY STAINTHORP BERGGREN

uniformed consistency across the screen. Then you press it onto a sheet — sort of a thick felt, that is damp — you press the screen from one side to the other trying to get an even sheet. Once the felt is full you place another piece of felt on it and keep pulling more sheets from the pulp. Once we had a good stack we needed to press the excess water out before hanging each sheet up to dry. This happened by placing a board on the stack of felt and uniforms and this guy hops in his old truck with his head out of the window guiding his front driver's side tire on the board and pushing the water out, squeezing it all over the pavement. Then we pulled the sheets of soon to be paper out and hung them with clothespins across a clothesline they'd set up for this purpose.

The uniforms dried like that, blowing in the wind on that cool May day.

While we were waiting on the sheets to settle we went back upstairs to the studio. I did a writing workshop with three or four other veterans, and we did a few exercises and were encouraged to read them out loud, and to consider the speaking of our written word as instrumental to the healing process as our written words could be.

The exercises we did involve one reading a poem by a young vet that served in Iraq, and responding to his poem. Another involved reading a poem by an Iraqi then writing a letter from the perspective of an Iraqi, and it could be addressed to anyone. The last exercise was sort of whimsical, like a dream. I wrote a letter from the Iraqi family who went to my friends to help dig up their young daughter that had been buried in the desert some time before at a mass gravesite. I wrote about tree houses and how if we could have a network of tree houses it might mean less homeless vets, and maybe when we got in them we'd feel like kids again. Maybe if we had tree houses we could forget some of the crap we were still carrying around.

I wrote about shame and anger; and guilt—and we all shared our writing and experiences with one another.

I remember my friend telling us about that Iraqi man he and his unit befriended and worked with in that village, but how the militia found out he was talking to the Marines. One day a black trash bag was thrown over the gates of his base, and in it was that man's head. I was glad he shared that and wondered about all the things he had been thinking when he was cutting all of his uniforms up. How it must have felt to turn those memories into paper, or how his paper felt now.

My paper felt thick and course.

My uniform was lightweight and smoother. I could put a set of cammies into a gallon size Ziploc bag. After I got out I still kept a pair in a Ziploc bag, and in a bin—I had two—one with my field supplies, another with my dress uniforms and accessories. I still have the bins with more of my shit in them—and I want to make more paper. We wrapped up and went to have beers for a while at this bar and we talked and talked and laughed. After the bar we went to my friends and sat in his backyard—around a big table—drinking and some smoking. We were still laughing and having a good time. Some of my friend's roommates got home and came outside too—so we talked a little about stuff we had done that day.

It was Memorial Day. It was a cool day in Chicago and one of the roommates chimed in during a lull in our conversations: "Have any of you lost any good friends?"

That didn't feel right, so I stayed quiet and looked down. My friend, who had led the writing exercises, then leaned over to me and said quietly "It amazes me the courage you all have but when this happens you all shut down." She always carried a lot of our weight and cared very deeply about every single one of us. I had tears in my eyes and I wanted those outsiders to leave, but we said nothing about it. It was Memorial Day and my paper, the day, my friends, it all felt right. Except that question. That felt like every other day.

BRIO

MAGGIE MARTIN

I have engaged the power of spring,
buzzing with life-force, ignorant of drought or death,
resilient as meadow grass and morning.
I sow community in re-acquisitioned places,
crowded city street, marching orders, protest song,
Our hands and mouths' unsinkable strength.
I have heard the rumble of feet on ground,
drum-beat depth, commencement of the connected,
roll on, advancing steady, through cities hungry,
stirring a hum in open heads and hearts.
Old constructs crumble and blow away,
new consciousness takes root.

REBUILDING: WARRIOR WRITERS IN ACTION

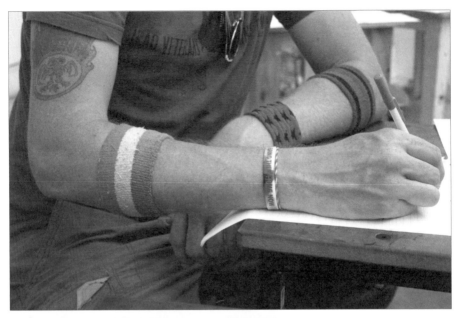

Above, Garett Reppenhagen writes at a workshop in Baltimore, Maryland, 2008.

Left, Drew Cameron and Evan Moodie write at a workshop in Burlington, Vermont, 2007.

Top Right, Eli Wright and Mike Blake write at a workshop in Newark, New Jersey, 2010.

Right, (from left) Aaron Hughes, Drew Cameron, Nick Morgan, and Ray Curry at a workshop in Baltimore, Maryland, 2008.

> *"I used to write before I went to Iraq, but when I got over there, I wasn't able to write. So through Warrior Writers I have been able to slowly begin to find my words again and share my experiences and what happened over there. It's been a healing experience."*
>
> Eli Wright
> Iraq Veteran, Warrior Writer

Above, veterans write at a Warrior Writers workshop during Winter Soldier in Silver Spring, Maryland, 2008. **Below,** (from left) Robynn Murray, Cherish Hodge, Nathan Lewis, David Mann, Jen Pacanowski and Hari Khalsa write at a workshop in Martha's Vineyard. **Top Right,** Jon Turner reads his work in 2007. **Bottom Right,** Jennifer Pacanowski performs in New York City, 2009.

> *"Yes we're going to rebuild. But it isn't rebuilding. Nothing can be made the same as before."*
>
> Maxine Hong Kingston
> Author, Warrior Writers
> Advisory Board

Above, Aaron Hughes prepares for the first Warrior Writers performance and book release at the Green Door Studio in Burlington, Vermont, 2007. **Below,** Drew Cameron performs in Baltimore, Maryland, 2008.

"It feels good to feel better."

Alex Ryabov
Iraq Veteran, Warrior Writer

AFTERWORD

JAMES A. MOAD II

As the son of a Vietnam Veteran, an Air Force pilot, and a Professor of War Literature, I've spent years trying to understand the disconnect between what a soldier is asked to do on the battlefield and the need for personal reconciliation in the aftermath of those experiences. The works presented on these pages represent an important and inspiring effort at bridging the divide between those who've experienced combat and a society distanced from the reality of war. The words and images are much more than the collective expressions of America's current generation of warriors — men and women who bear the physical and mental scars of war — they're also powerful testimonials to future generations about the individual cost of war.

From *The Odyssey* to *A Farewell to Arms* and from *The Deer Hunter* to *The Hurt Locker*, the literary and artistic expressions of war remind us how the lingering trauma of combat transcends the individual experience. It resonates throughout society and across generations, informing us all of the need to engage in the healing process as a nation. Art, after all, is ultimately about sharing — images, words, and stories to capture the essence of an emotion or experience and convey that which defies simple explanations. For the individual, healing and reconciliation are often about acceptance and understanding, efforts rendered by actively confronting the experiences of war, and expressing the boxed up pain within.

A few years ago I was introduced to the Warrior Writers at a conference in Denver. Impressed by their commitment to our nation's soldiers, I decided to attend one of their seminars this past spring. A few months before I'd undergone reconstructive shoulder surgery and was on medical leave from my job as an airline pilot. There were complications with the surgery, and I wasn't certain if I'd ever get back into the cockpit again. Shortly before the seminar, despite intensive physical therapy, I stopped making progress. I kept pushing myself, but as my doctor reminded me, the surgery was incredibly traumatic (four different procedures rolled into one). The muscles all around my shoulder, back and side had contracted, limiting my range of motion. The scars had healed, but my muscles were locked into a protective mode, as if they were afraid I might damage it again. I was frustrated, and while attending the conference, I took part in a Reiki session (a form of energy transfer in the body) offered to those in attendance. Following the session, I began to feel a shift within me. After consulting with the therapist, I decided to add massage therapy to help my muscles let go of the tension. After a few sessions, the muscles began to relax, allowing my range to gradually return until I was able to pass my flight physical.

While I was surprised at this new path to recovery, I shouldn't have been. The Warrior Writers are all about using creative energy to help Vets confront the trauma of war through artistic expression. I realize that my own limitations were tied to the muscle memory—a powerful force that limited my ability to recover and reach my potential. Of course, for many Vets and victims of trauma, the memory of pain is what keeps them from healing. By having them write, draw, or mold their experiences into art, the pain and anger boxed up within them loses part of its destructive character. They can, like all artists, give themselves over to the power of imagination—an effort which both frees and creates a new way of seeing and engaging their own experiences.

BIOGRAPHIES

Aikens, Tom: Tom served in the military from 2001 to 2005. He served with the Army and deployed to Kosovo from 2002 to 2003. Tom was with 2-2 INF 1st ID when he deployed for OIF (Operation Iraqi Freedom) II. He primarily writes poetry as a means of defining the issues that linger so he can work through them and master them. Tom is also trying to reintegrate aspects of self into his life in a manner that does not allow them to define him.

Anthony Michael: Michael served six years in the Army Reserves as an operating room technician and was deployed to Mosul and Al Asad in Iraq for twelve months. After returning, he published a memoir detailing his war experiences, *Mass Casualties: A Young Medic's True Story of Death, Deception and Dishonor in Iraq*. He is now a senior in college earning his Bachelor's Degree in English with a concentration in creative writing.

Bateman, Chantelle: Chantelle is a former Marine and longtime writer who has found Warrior Writers to be an important part of her healing process. She served in Al Asad, Iraq with MAG16 Forward from 2004 to 2005. She is currently an organizer with Iraq Veterans Against the War (IVAW) working to help other veterans unpack their military experiences and build healing communities working for change.

Beck, Brennan: Brennan served with the Army in the infantry from 2005 to 2010. He served two combat deployments to Iraq. The first was in Baghdad from 2006 to 2007 and the second was in Mahawil from 2008 to 2009. Brennan left the Army as Sergeant in February of 2010 to go to college. He started writing as therapy after coming home from his second deployment.

Beining, Sarah: Sarah served in the Army from 2004 to 2007. She spent 2006 in Baghdad and ended her time in the Army after returning from the deployment. Sarah was a 96B, Intelligence Analyst for the 4ID out of Ft. Hood, Texas. She is now a writer and divorced mother of one beautiful little girl and tutors writing students at Indiana-Purdue University, Ft. Wayne, IN.

Cameron, Drew: Drew served in the Army from 2000 to 2004. He is an Iraq War veteran, having served with 6th Battalion 27th Field Artillery Regiment. Following his deployment Drew served two years in the Vermont Army National Guard and was medically separated in 2006. A co-founder of the Combat Paper Project, he is a hand papermaker who practices and teaches the traditional craft and works on encouraging others to do the same.

Camper, Raymond: Ray served in the Virginia and Minnesota Army National Guard from 2003 to 2009 as a chaplain's assistant and administration specialist. He deployed to Iraq with the 434th MSB from 2005 to 2007, functioning primary within the roles of base security and force protection. Ray enjoys writing, and has found his interactions with Warrior Writers therapeutic and liberating.

Casey, Sean: Sean Casey is originally from Lowell, MA. After graduating from Miami University (OH), Sean enlisted in the Army and spent the next five years leading and training soldiers as a Cavalry officer. During Sean's five years, he was deployed to Baghdad, Iraq in 2006 and 2009. Sean continues his military life today as a public affairs officer in the Army Reserve. Much of Sean's published writing revolves around his military experiences. He feels that writing brings "order to the internal chaos."

Cliburn, Justin: Justin deployed to Iraq from 2005 to 2006 with the Oklahoma Army National Guard. He served as a Humvee gunner in a squad that escorted State Department police officers to and from Iraqi police stations in Baghdad. His squad was responsible for helping train Iraqi police. He is now married and attending the University of Oklahoma College of Law.

Clumpner, Graham: Graham served in the Army with 2/75 RGR RGT from 2004 to 2007 and deployed for OEF in Afghanistan/Pakistan. He believes that "People should not be afraid of their governments. Government's should be afraid of their people."

Conerd, Dan: Dan served in the Army from 2003 to 2007. He deployed to Iraq in 2005. He served as a heavy construction operator with the 94th Engineers. Dan started his own clothing line Alternate Decision Clothing and he is currently planning on opening up his own store-front in downtown Denver. You may visit his website at alternatedecision.com.

Covell, Stephen: Stephen served four years in the Army as a combat medic from 2006 to 2010. Aside from training, he spent his entire enlistment assigned to a recon squadron in the 82nd Airborne Division and deployed twice to Iraq in 2007 and 2009. He currently is a songwriter and performer.

Covington, P.W.: P.W. served in the Air Force and the Air Force Reserve from 1992 to 2004 as an air transportation specialist, on combat missions in Afghanistan, Southwest Asia, and East Africa. A service-connected disabled veteran, he works with fellow veterans in South Texas as a peer facilitator. He is the author of a poetry collection, *Like the Prayers of an Infidel*.

Daley, Jim: Jim served five years active and twelve years as a reservist. He served as a Navy Corpsman with the 1st Marine Division based out of Camp Fallujah in 2004.

Day, Michael: Michael is a Marine combat veteran. He rests his head in Manhattan and is fascinated by the idea that each syllable that he writes will bring him closer to _____.

Dean, Zachariah: Zachariah is a Marine reservist who served with part of Bravo Company, 4th Combat Engineer Battalion. Dean spent the majority of 2010 serving under OEF in Sangin, Afghanistan sweeping for IED's and performing demolition. He currently resides in Harrisonburg, VA with his dog Gatsby.

Doherty, Patrick Majid: Patrick served in the Army and was discharged at the rank of Private after three plus years of service. He was stationed in Manheim for 30 days and was court martialed. Patrick has studied writing at the William Joiner Center for the Study of War and Social Consequences of University of Massachusetts in Boston. His discharge was upgraded to honorable.

Dougherty, Kelly: Kelly was in the Army National Guard, and deployed with the 220th Military Police unit from the Colorado Army National Guard. She also served as a medic in Det. 5 medical unit. Kelly served in Colorado, Hungary, Croatia, Iraq, and Kuwait.

Ekstrom, Lars: Lars, a strong supporter of the Iraq War, reported to boot camp in 2003, six months after graduating high school. His faith in the military and the mission of the U.S., however, steadily eroded during his training and subsequent deployment to Iraq. The young corporal became troubled by a lack of accountability on the part of a culture he says is too "indoctrinated" to reform itself. After his discharge, Lars waited six months for Veterans Administration benefits and continues to overcome bureaucratic obstacles as he seeks treatment for his depression.

Estenzo, Eric: Eric is a career artist based in Rhode Island. He served six years in the Marines with 4th Light Armored Reconnaissance Battalion from 1999 to 2005. Eric is currently living in Rhode Island and attending the Rhode Island School of Design.

Feliciano, Iris M.: The focus of Iris' work is on creative expression as a medium for social consciousness. She says, "I was not socially conscious when I deployed for OEF in 2002. I was not fully informed when I joined the Marine Corps. It was not until I returned home to Chicago that I began to see that, indeed, war touches all of our lives and that there is, in fact, no freedom to be endured. On the streets…there is evidence of the dysfunction caused by war and violence. My only hope is to capture this reality in my writing and photography in order to try to make sense of a world that no longer does."

Figueroa, Mario: Mario is a former Marine and combat veteran of OIF II. He served with 2nd Battalion 7th Marines as an infantry squad leader, team leader and radio operator. Mario is currently a student at Columbia University in New York City.

Foote, Frederick: Frederick served in the Navy Medical Corps in Iraq. His poetry and prose have been published in the *Journal of the American Medical Association,* the *Progressive, Commonweal: A Review of Religion, Politics and Culture,* and other publications.

George, Jacob: Jacob served in the Army with 528th SOSB as a combat engineer. He served three tours in OEF from 2001 to 2004.

Goodwin, Nicole: Nicole was one of the first homeless veterans of the Iraq War and was featured in the documentary "When I Came Home," as well as many news programs. She lives in New York City where she raises her daughter, writes poetry, and attends college.

Gubbins, Vartan: Vartan served in the Army Reserve from 2000 to 2008. He deployed to Iraq from 2004 to 2005. He loves writing poetry about anything, but especially about war.

Hartbarger, Toby: Toby served in the Army from 2002 to 2004. He deployed to Iraq from 2003 to 2004 as an infantry/mortar man.

Herrera, Amy: Amy served in the Air Force as a Weather Journeyman from 2001 to 2005. She was stationed at SAFB, IL. Amy has a Master's in Public Administration with an emphasis in government business relations and NP policy.

Hodge, Cherish: Cherish joined the Army in an attempt to serve her nation and those abroad. It wasn't until she was at her first duty station that she realized each military code, value and ethic imbued into the young minds of soldiers was a lie. After separation from the military, Cherish began working with organizations to try to bring an end to war, provide veterans with appropriate care and educate the public on the prevarication that continues in our military. She lives in Ventura, CA with her son Ocean and is studying medicine to continue the dedication of service to her nation and those abroad.

Hughes, Aaron: Aaron was called to active duty in 2003 with the 1244th Transportation Company Army National Guard out of Illinois and was deployed to Kuwait during OIF, supporting combat operations by transporting supplies from camps and ports in Kuwait to camps in Iraq. After three extensions, totaling one year, three months and seven days, Aaron returned to the University of Illinois in 2005 as a student majoring in painting with the need to express and share his experiences with others. It was there he began to use art as a tool to confront issues of militarism and occupation.

Inzunza, Victor: Victor served on active duty from 2001 to 2005 with the Marines. He served with 1st battalion 2nd Marines as a field wireman. Victor was present at the Battle of Nasiriya during the invasion of Iraq in 2003, which has become an inspiration for much of his writing. He returned for a second deployment in 2004 to Iskandiriyah, Iraq. He studied English and Creative Writing at University of the Pacific in Stockton, CA, where he now lives with his wife Heather and son Cadence.

Key, Jeff: Jeff is a former Marine Iraq veteran, playwright, poet, peace activist, and queer civil rights activist. He is the author and performer of the award winning play *The Eyes of Babylon* and is the founding board member of The Mehadi Foundation which provides support for returning veterans and philanthropic projects including supplying clean water and other basic necessities to citizens in Iraq and Afghanistan. (theeyesofbabylon.com, MehadiFoundation.org)

Kilgore, Kevin: Kevin served in the Marines from 1993 to 1997 as a data processor, the United States Army Reserve from 1997 to 1999, the United States Naval Reserve from 1999 to 2000 as a steel worker, and the Texas Air National Guard from 2000 to 2003 in public affairs. He was part of Task Force Confidence (Dallas/Ft. Worth) from 2001 to 2002. Kevin received five additional medals because of 9-11, without leaving the United States or doing anything daring.

Kochergin, Sergio: Sergio is from Holland, PA and joined the Marines in 2002. He deployed with the main invading force with 1st Bn 7th Mar A co 3 platoon Combat Team and spent the rest of his tour in An Najaf. He then redeployed 2004 to Husaybah on the Syrian border. Sergio joined IVAW in 2007 and has been a member since.

Kyrie, Ash: Ash has not quite filled his dream to live off the grid. Read more at: ashkyrie.com.

Lambert, Fred: Fred served in the Marines as a rifleman from 2002 to 2006, including two tours in Iraq as a member of 1St Marine Division's India Company, Third battalion, Fifth Marines; the first in 2003 and the second in 2004-2005. Fred received a Navy and Marine Corps Commendation Medal with a Combat "V" for valor in Fallujah, and he currently writes for the *Valencia Voice*, a college news publication of Valencia College in Orlando, FL.

Lara, Jonas: Jonas served in the Marines as a mortar man from 2000 to 2003. After becoming injured while training for deployment he was medically discharged. Feeling a sense of guilt for not being with his Marines in Iraq while also dealing with multiple injuries, Lara needed an outlet to express himself so he enrolled at the Art Center College of Design in Pasadena, CA and received a Bachelor's of Fine Art in Photography and Imaging in 2009. He is currently working on his Master's degree in Fine Art at the School of Visual Art in New York City.

LaPorte, Zach: Zach served with the 2nd Battalion 75th Ranger regiment in conjunction with the U.S. Special Operation Command from 2004 to 2007. He served two deployments as part of a machine gun team in support of OIF. Zach now lives and works in Milwaukee, WI as a mechanical engineer.

LaSalla Booker, Sarah: Sarah joined the Marine Corps prior to 9/11. After the attacks, she shipped out with the 22nd MEU and served in OEF. She currently holds a Bachelor's in English Literature from Rockford College. She has been a writer and poet all her life, received collegiate awards for her work and creates visual art, working typically with pencils or acrylics.

LaVallee, Ian: Ian served in the Army in B co. 2-325 AIR, 82nd Airborne Division as an Airborne infantryman. He deployed to Tal Afar, Iraq in 2005. Ian's passions now include Massage Therapy/Energy Therapies, community organizing, sustainable food systems, wild crafting and hunting, being in the wilderness, and reconnecting with his Brazilian roots.

Lewis, Nathan: Nate joined the Army straight out of high school. September 11, 2001, was his second day of boot camp. He deployed to Iraq in 2003. Nate joined IVAW after he got out and obtained a degree in History and Secondary Social Sciences from the State University of New York at Potsdam. He also played a role of a U.S. soldier in the movie about the Iraq war called *Green Zone*. Nathan is the author of a poetry collection entitled *I Hacky Sacked in Iraq* (Combat PaperPress, 2009).

Madden, Liam: Liam was a Sergeant in the Marines, serving from 2003 to 2007. A tactical communications specialist, he served in Iraq from 2004 to 2005. After returning from Iraq, Liam organized the Appeal for Redress, which enabled service members to voice their opposition to the war in Iraq. He was given adverse fitness reports as a consequence of political activities. Today Liam is working to build sustainable urban food and energy systems. He writes and speaks about sacred economics, the transformation of civilization into a community based on the giving of our unique and needed gifts.

Mann, David: David, a Specialist in the Army served as a radio communications security repairer in OEF and OIF I in An Nasiryah and Kuwait. In OIF III he served in Balad. He was also stationed at Ft. Carson, CO. As a lover of life and the overall human experience, he never supported the war and spent two deployments anguishing over his personal contribution to the war in Iraq. After getting out, David got involved with IVAW and subsequently found that writing his experiences down and sharing with other people was a great part of his healing process.

Martin, Maggie: Maggie served in the Army from 2001 to 2006. She deployed to Kuwait before the war and twice to Iraq in 2003 and 2005 with the 3rd Infantry Division as a Signal. A Sergeant in the Army Signal Corps, Maggie also served at Ft. Stewart, GA.

McNeill, Rachel: Rachel served as a heavy construction equipment operator in the Army Reserve's 826th Ordnance Company from 2002 to 2010 in Madison, WI. She deployed with the 983rd Engineer Battalion for OIF III from 2004 to 2005 where she served as a driver and turret gunner on convoys throughout Anbar Province. She has testified before the Senate Democratic Policy Committee about contractor misconduct and was featured in the book *The Girls Come Marching Home: Stories of Women Warriors Returning from the War in Iraq*. Rachel was medically retired as a Sergeant and is now a degree candidate at Harvard University Extension School and active member of the Smedley D. Butler Brigade of Veterans for Peace (VFP) in Boston, MA.

Millard, Geoff: Due to the attacks on the World Trade Center of September 11, 2001 Geoff, as a member of the 42nd Infantry Division, was activated and given ground zero security missions. In 2004 Sgt. Millard was activated with the 42nd ID ROC to participate in thirteen months of OIF II. Geoff taught American pluralism at SUNY Buffalo and earned a BA in American studies in May of 2009.

Mizula, Jason: Jason served four years with the Coast Guard on active duty as a Petty Officer 3rd Class, doing counter narcotic and immigration patrols in the Caribbean & eastern Pacific, working with Fisheries in the North Atlantic and helping with New Orleans Katrina relief in 2005. He also served two years in the Army National Guard as a Specialist and deployed with C-Co 1-181 26th Infantry Yankee Division for OIF III from 2007 to 2008 Jason was honorably discharged from both branches. He is currently a member of VFP, IVAW, and Iraq and Afghanistan Veterans of America (IAVA).

Moad II, James: Jay is a former Air Force C-130 pilot with over 3000 hours of flight time, and over a hundred combat sorties. He is a graduate of the Air Force Academy where he later served as a professor of war literature and as a fiction editor for the international journal, *War, Literature and the Arts (WLA)*. He also blogs for *WLA* at wlajournal.com/blog.

Morgan, Nick: Nick served in the Army Reserve as an engineer from 2002 to 2006. He was deployed to Baghdad, Iraq from 2004 to 2005 and served under the 1st Calvary Division. In 2008 he suffered severe facial injuries at the hands of the Nassau County Police Department in Hempstead, NY while demanding veterans' voices be heard at the final presidential debate between John McCain and Barrack Obama.

Muncy, Malachi: Malachi served in the Texas National Guard from 2003 to 2009 and deployed to Iraq from 2004 to 2005 and 2006 to 2007. A journalism student at Texas State University, in 2011 he founded Button Field Press, a paper studio that works with service members, veterans, and communities affected by violence

Murray, Robynn: Robynn joined the Army Reserve in 2003 and deployed to Iraq in 2004 with the 403rd Civil Affairs Battalion. She served as her team's machine gunner and worked security detail. She's an active member of IVAW and participated in Winter Soldier 2008 to get veterans stories out to the public. She was recently featured in the 2011 HBO documentary *Poster Girl*.

Newsom, Aaron: Aaron served in the Marines from 2002 to 2008 as an expeditionary aircraft recovery specialist. He was deployed to Afghanistan from 2004 to 2005. Aaron is currently a member of IVAW, VFP, and The Farmer Veteran Coalition. He writes because it helps him express the frustration, anger, pain, and mental anguish of his days in war.

Pacanowski, Jennifer: Jen is an Iraq War veteran that served in the Army as a combat medic from 2003 to 2005. After her experiences in the war she was left dealing with severe PTSD, addiction, and anger. During a Warrior Writers' retreat, she found solace and healing in making art. She resides in Ithaca, NY where she facilitates writing workshops for Veteran's Sanctuary, an organization that provides holistic healing, art programs and peer support for veterans.

Palumbo, Charlie: Charlie is a female veteran who served in the Navy in Yokosuka, Japan from 1998 to 2002. Her passion is to serve the veteran community through arts and activism. She has recently authored her first book, *The Face of a Memory* and donates 80% of her proceeds to Give an Hour.

Reinholdt, Bryan: Despite being disillusioned by the Army Reserve system and its readiness, Bryan deployed with 8/229 Aviation Regiment under the 42nd Infantry Division in 2004, serving as an Apache helicopter electrical and armament system specialist. The deployment in support of OIF III shed light on the operational function of the unit, but the experience also challenged him to rethink the purposes and motives for war. In 2007 Bryan completed his visual arts and arts education degree at Bellarmine University and served out his time in the military.

Reppenhagen, Garett: Garett enlisted in 2001 as a Cavalry Scout with the Army. He served in Germany and on a peace-keeping mission in Kosovo in 2002-2003. He deployed to Iraq in 2004 and was stationed at forward operating base Scunion near Baquaba doing sniper missions in the Diyala region. Garett co-authored the anti-war blog *Fight To Survive* and joined IVAW as the first active duty member in 2004. He was stop-lossed for ten months and honorably discharged in 2005. Garett worked as the VP of Public Relations for Nobel Prize winning Veterans for America and remains a veteran advocate.

Scranton, Roy: Roy served in Iraq from 2003 to 2004 with C 1/94 FA (MLRS/TA), 1st AD. He writes fiction, poetry, and essays that have been published in *The Massachusetts Review*, *New Letters*, *LIT*, *The New York Times*, *Theory & Event*, and elsewhere. Roy is currently earning a PhD in English at Princeton.

Stainthorp Berggren, Jeremy: Jeremy served in the Marine Reserves from 1998 to 2006. He was trained in supply and in 2003 his unit was trained in mortuary affairs. In 2001 a member of his unit committed suicide and he uses art and writing to express his experiences and feelings towards that specific event and military suicide as a systemic problem.

Stone, Amber: Amber served in the Army from 2003 to 2009 as a combat medic. She deployed to Iraq for one year during OIF III. She is still fighting the fight; not just for herself, but also for her fellow veterans.

Sullivan, Peter: Peter served in the Army National Guard for twelve years as an infantry soldier. He has been drawing and making art since he was about five years old.

Turner, Jon: Jon has used creation as a mechanism to find healing through divine inner thought. Having suffered the realities of disillusionment as an infantryman in the Marines, his experience is found in scribbles left on handmade paper.

Valencia, Jesse Michael-Geronimo: Jesse served in the Army Reserve from 2006 to 2011, but was never deployed due to service-related injuries. Jesse was a military police officer based out of Mesa, AZ.

Viges, Hart: Hart is an American nomad born in Phoenix who joined the Army in reaction to 9-11. Hart served with the 82nd Airborne Division 1/325 as a mortar man in Iraq from 2003 to 2004. After returning, he filed for conscientious objector (CO) status and received an honorable discharge. He is now a Chaplain with IVAW and an active Counter-Recruiter. Hart lives in San Angelo, TX and is earning a degree in Communication so he can become a high school teacher.

Vogt, Kristina: Kristine served in the Air Force in 2005. She is currently a graduate student studying Acupuncture and Herbs at Pacific College of Oriental Medicine at the NY campus.

Wagner, Joyce: Joyce served in the Marine Corps from 2002 to 2006 as an avionics technician on attack and reconnaissance helicopters. She was deployed to Iraq in 2004 and 2005. She was the first woman in her shop and one of the first two women to serve at Camp Korean Village in Iraq. Joyce is a multidisciplinary artist who combines video, sculpture, print, and salvaged materials and frequently addresses themes of gender and gender roles, reproduction, and militarism.

Wasserman, Paul: Paul served in the Army as a Staff Sergeant with an aircrew in Iraq. He published a volume of poems last spring, *Say Again All*, based on his time in country. Currently he is a PhD candidate and a teacher. Paul is also working on a war novel.

Weselowski, Kyle: Kyle served in the Army with the 1/12 Calvary 3rd Brigade as a tank crew member. He is the contact for the Ft. Hood chapter of IVAW.

White, Josiah: Josiah joined the Marines in June of 2005 and was medically retired in 2008 after being severely wounded by a suicide bomber. He studies physics and writing in San Diego, CA with his wife Yohanna.

Wright, Eli: An Army combat medic from 2002 to 2008, including service in Iraq in 2003 to 2004, Eli began working with Warrior Writers and Combat Paper Project while on active duty. He is co-director of papermaking workshops for veterans at the Printmaking Council of NJ.

Yates, Emily: Emily is an Army veteran who served six years, including two combat tours to Iraq, as a public affairs specialist, military journalist and photographer. Through photography, she realized the therapeutic effect of art in her transition from soldier to civilian. This prompted her to help create Veteran Artists (www.veteranartists.org), a non-profit that helps veterans achieve their artistic goals without any cost to them. She lives in Oakland, CA, and is completing a bachelor's degree in near eastern studies at the University of California, Berkeley.

Yoczik, Steve: Steve was a network switching systems operator/maintainer in the Army and was stationed at Ft. Gordon, GA. He never deployed and after a year of trying to get out, Steve went Absent Without Leave (AWOL) to Canada for about two and a half years before turning himself in. He realized his obligation to resist once he heard stories from returning veterans.

Zabel, Tyler: Tyler served with the Army National Guard for four years and did not deploy. His unit was 11 Bravo/Infantry. Tyler was a Specialist, but was bumped down to PV2 after going AWOL. He was released as a CO.

INDEX

ACKNOWLEDGEMENTS

This book would not be in your hands without the work of each and every artist whose voice and perspective make this book the powerful collection that it is. There were also many others who helped us with the nitty-gritty details and we appreciate all their work too. Thank you all very much!

Editorial Collective: Jan Barry, Michael Day, Iris Feliciano, Rachel McNeill, Emily Yates

Guest Editors: Caroline DeLuca, Dan Gleason, Nicole Goodwin, Toby Hartbarger, Nan Levinson, Maggie Martin, Peter Sullivan

Copy Editors: Jan Barry, Michael Gillen, Bryon Reiger, Josiah White

Warrior Writers' Staff: Lovella Calica, Jamie DeAngelis, Lily Hughes, Lynn Estomin, Irit Reinheimer, Meaghan F. Washington

Warrior Writers' Steering Committee: Stephen Funk, Maggie Martin, Rachel McNeill, Jen Pacanowski, Bryan Reindholt, Andy Sapp

Warrior Writers' Advisory Board: Jan Barry, Stacey Engels, Lynn Estomin, Tony Heriza, Maxine Hong Kingston, Sara Nesson, Ward Reilly, Ted Sexauer, Lamont Steptoe

Others who helped get submissions, provided logistical support, etc.: Iraq Veterans Against The War, NYU Veterans Writing Workshop, Veteran Photography Workshop, Reclaim Print Shop, Studio 34, Brian Turner, Jay Moad II, L. Brown and Sons Printing, Inc., Combat Paper Project, Veterans Sanctuary, Under The Hood, and many, many more.

A big thank you to all of our Kickstarter Fundraising Campaign supporters!

"When you write the pain of war, you will relive it.
You're going to live through the pain again.
You do relive the war, the emotions, the smells.
But this time you have a method for handling it — writing.
You can control it, put it down, pick it up.
Writing is a craft of the hand."

Larry Heinemann, Vietnam Veteran, Author

WARRIOR*Writers*